T0067913

Words of John,
Thoughts of God

Words of John, *Thoughts of God*

Devotions on the Epistles of
St. John the Beloved

MIKE RAMEY

Archway Publishing books may be ordered through booksellers or by contacting:

Archway Publishing
1663 Liberty Drive
Bloomington, IN 47403
www.archwaypublishing.com
844-669-3957

ISBN: 978-1-6657-3717-3 (sc)
ISBN: 978-1-6657-3718-0 (e)

Library of Congress Control Number: 2023900839

Print information available on the last page.

Archway Publishing rev. date: 02/01/2023

Introduction

St. John is known by several designations: he is the son of Zebedee, the brother of James, and is referred to as "the beloved disciple" or "the disciple Jesus loved." He was known as the writer of the Gospel and Epistles that bear his name, along with the Book of Revelation as affirmed by Polycarp (70-156 AD) and Pappias (70-146 AD). The early Church Fathers, Irenaeus (120-202 AD), Justin Martyr (110-165 AD), and Tertullian (145-220 AD) all ascribe to John's apostleship and authorship of the aforementioned writings. John's writings are traditionally ascribed to his later years as he, the "elder," writes to younger Christians (not necessarily chronologically younger) to help them oppose the false teachings and teachers who had questions the dual nature of Christ, as well as His redemptive work.

John writes in simple Greek but speaks of deep issues of faith and practice. Unlike traditional "letters," his epistles read like a sermon from a father-teacher to his children-students. As we hear his words, we are given privy to the very thoughts of God, shared in the "truth and love" characteristic of John's writings.

Eugene Peterson writes in his introduction to John's epistles in *The Message* that "The basic and biblical Christian conviction is that the two subjects [love and God] are intricately related. If we want to deal with God the right way, we have to learn to love the right way. If we want to love the right way, we have to deal with God the right way. God and love can't be separated. John's three letters provide wonderfully explicit directions in how this works."[1]

With Jesus as the focal point of our faith, God and love come together, are embodied in His Person, and are lived out in the lives of those who bear His name. It's all about Jesus who makes God's love real for us.

---

[1] Eugene Peterson, *The Message: The Bible in Contemporary Language*, © 2002 by Eugene Peterson. Used by permission of NavPress Publishing Group, p. 2222.

1 John 1:1, $_{MSG}$

"From the very first day, we were there, taking it all in - we heard it with our own ears, saw it with our own eyes, verified it with our own hands."

Witnesses. Testimonies. Affidavits. Depositions. If we have ever been involved in a legal proceeding or if we have watched courtroom procedural dramas, these terms are familiar to us. The witness is called to the stand to give their testimony as to what they saw or heard. There may be a cross-examination and perhaps, a rebuttal – or not. But their words become part of the written record. "Do you swear to give the truth, the whole truth, and nothing but the truth, so help you God?" The testimony of witnesses is used to both convict and exonerate the accused. Their words have power; they affect the lives of others.

St. John the Beloved sits on Patmos in exile for being a Christian. He had been pastor in Ephesus for many years prior. Unlike the rest of the original, apostolic group, he had not been put to death but sent into exile. He is the last of the original apostles, and he writes as "the elder" to a second generation of believers. He is testifying to Jesus as one of the last surviving men to have personally seen, heard, and experienced the Son of God while He walked upon the earth. His witness is crucial, for false teachers were busily teaching false teachings (after all, that's what they do, right?). Some taught that Jesus was God who only appeared to be a man; others submitted that Christ was a man used by God for a time. John's testimony is a direct rebuttal to them all: "I was there. I saw Him. I heard Him. I watched Him. I touched Him. Let me tell you the true story!"

There are a number of historic figures who verify who John was despite the clamor of those who question his identity and his validity. The courtroom has been called to order and John takes the stand. In the face of accusations, we are going to hear John's words speak God's thoughts as the Spirit moves "the beloved disciple" to tell us the truth about Jesus.

Prayer: Holy God, move us to approach our Bible as the testimony of witnesses and evangelists and prophets who wrote at Your beckoning. As we hear John speak, move us to hear You and to believe him as the witness to truth and love that You called him to be. Let his words move us to love and to believe as You would have us to live; through Jesus Christ, our Lord. Amen.

1 John 1:2 *MSG*

"The Word of Life appeared right before our eyes; we saw it happen! And now we're telling you in most sober prose that what we witnessed was, incredibly, this: The infinite Life of God himself took shape before us."

Years ago we took a trip to Disneyworld with the kids. Because it was going to be the one, major family vacation we'd ever take, I encouraged my wife to research all the options and opportunities that would be available to us – where to stay, what food venues to eat at, what shows to go to. One choice caught me off guard; she booked us (for over $300) to see the Cirque de Soleil. Now, I don't mind a good circus, but I couldn't fathom what kinds of elephants, lions, tigers, bears, and clowns would be worth such expense. I balked, but she explained, "It's not that kind of a circus." And it wasn't. I cannot adequately describe the experience with words – you just had to be there!

"The Word of life appeared right before our eyes; we saw it happen!" John is sharing his personal testimony of the God-event of Jesus. "Don't listen to what others are saying, they weren't there, but I was!" The new generation of believers were facing false teachers that questioned the Gospel. "Was Jesus man or God? Can He be both?" Some were swayed by their deceptions. Fewer and fewer people who had seen Jesus were alive. John is the last of the apostles and he was a very old. "...we saw it happen. And now we're telling you in most sober prose that what we witnessed was, incredibly, this: The infinite Life of God himself took shape before us." John was challenging the false teachers directly; it was as if he were saying, "Jesus is more than a man, He's the very God Himself. I experienced Him as He taught and healed and sacrificed and died and was raised from the dead. You don't get it – you just had to be there!"

The Church continued to struggle with the question of the "Who" and the "What" of Jesus for hundreds of years. It still does today. The second and third generations of believers sought to crystalize the teachings about Jesus by stating unequivocally their faith with the Apostles' Creed, written as a summary of the teachings of the apostles. Later, they would face down the false notions at Nicaea (325 AD) and produce the confession of the Nicene Creed – again based on the testimonies of John and the others who had shared their eyewitness accounts. "We saw it happen!" You just had to be there!

Prayer: Holy Father, who sent Jesus to be our Savior as the very "Life of God," we hearken to the words of those who saw Him and knew Him. We weren't there; but they were. Help us to receive their testimony with the Holy Spirit's indwelling presence that we come and grow in saving faith; through Jesus Christ our Lord. Amen.

1 John 1:3-4, MSG

"We saw it, we heard it, and now we're telling you so you can experience it along with us, this experience of communion with the Father and with his Son, Jesus Christ. Our motive for writing is simply this: We want you to enjoy this, too. Your joy will double our joy!"

Cynical by nature, sarcastic from practice, I have to admit that I often look for the ulterior motives of people. I want to know what they get out of things. When someone tries to persuade me to try something, I wonder if maybe they will profit in some fashion or if they have a stake in the product, they're pushing on me. "Here, try this!" is often met the with question mark over my head – "Why? What's it to you?"

John is writing to an audience of believers being discouraged to continue in the faith as it had been taught to them. Questions led to doubts that led to confusion; what they thought they knew was no longer a certainty to them. Some were being misled; others were throwing their hands up in surrender and walking away. But John calls out to them, encouraging believers: "We saw it, we heard it, and now we're telling you so you can experience it along with us, this experience of communion with the Father and his Son, Jesus Christ." The elder apostle is inviting his children in the faith to enjoy what he has – a relationships with the Almighty that is made possible and available through Jesus. John's life and testimony revolved around Jesus. Ever since that day in Galilee, when He had invited the brothers Zebedee to "Follow Me," John had. His brother, James, was murdered early on because of his faith. John had winced at the reports of the deaths of his friends and traveling companions. He was exiled on Patmos, cut off from his church family at Ephesus. One might have been inclined to question his motives: "What do you get out of this, old man?

What's it to you?" John answers the skepticism: "Our motive for writing to you is simply this: We want you to enjoy this too. You joy will double our joy."

Not everyone is trying to separate you from your money; not everything is meant as a "come-on" or enticement to indulge. The apostle is not peddling the Gospel "for a donation of $20 to my ministry." Set aside the cynicism for John's motivation to write is genuine: "We [just] want you to enjoy this too."

Prayer: Lord God Almighty, though You willingly offered Your Son's life for our sins and our salvation, it was to reunite us unto the relationship You wanted to have with us from all eternity. May we see Your gifts as they are – gifts – and may be led by Your Spirit to joyfully commune with You; through Jesus Christ, Your Son, our Lord, who with You and the Holy Spirit are the one, true God, forever and ever. Amen.

1 John 1:5, MSG

"This, in essence, is the message we heard from Christ and are passing on to you: God is light, pure light; there's not a trace of darkness in him."

John often speaks in terms of stark contrasts, such as "light versus darkness." For him, as for us, it's important that we understand that there is a separation between "light" and "darkness," just as there is no comingling between "truth" and "lies." Many people try to live in the middle; living enough in the light to keep out of the shadows, but sometimes venturing into the darkness just to see what's going on there. Some want to live in "truth," but often they devise a personal sense of truth that meets their pre-determined narrative; it's "their truth" that works for them, but not necessarily for everyone else. We bristle at the "either/or" delineations and desire the "both/and" solutions, but that is not always feasible: You're either alive or you're not – zombies do not exist in the realm of reality.

"God is light, pure light; there's not a trace of darkness in him." Since we cannot imagine true purity, it is hard for us to grasp the concept. While we like to think of the pure innocence of children, the experienced parent knows better. Nothing demonstrates the sinful condition of the children of men like a toddler throwing a tantrum when they don't get their way! Most advertisers will say their product is 99.9% effective because they know of circumstances where it won't work. Purity may be longed-for and celebrated, but it is too easily stained and sullied among men. Not so with God. He is "pure light; there's not a trace of darkness in him."

"God is light" which implies that we're not. That is quite humbling since it means we cannot measure up to God's standards or expectations. We "miss the mark" – i.e., we sin. Some will want to rebel, either seeking to tarnish God's "glow" ("What kind of a God would…?") or they will gloss over their personal stains ("After all, no one's perfect!"). But nothing changes that stark contrast between God and the children of men except when He who is pure seeks to make pure those who are not.

Prayer: Holy God, we, the unholy children of men, stand before You in awe. Unable to naturally meet Your expectations or appease Your justice, we are at Your mercy. But Your mercy is there for us and for all in Christ Jesus. Repentant and faithful, move us by Your mercy to the cross where our stains are blotted out by His blood. Amen.

1 John 1:6-7, MSG

"If we claim that we experience a shared life with him and continue to stumble around in the dark, we're obviously lying through our teeth - we're not living as we claim. But if we walk in light, God himself being the light, we also experience a shared life with one another, as the sacrificial blood of Jesus, God's Son, purges all our sin."

The stark contrast of being creatures of light trying to navigate in the dark is best experienced when you're up in the "wee hours," trying to not wake your spouse as you make your way across the bedroom, finding every bump and tripping hazard between the bed and the bathroom. In the dark, it's hard to get your bearings. What looks look a clear path turns out to be the dresser. You thought the step was only two inches high, but your now-throbbing toe discovered it was four. You reach your destination, but there's the return trip. Too bad they don't make steel-toed slippers!

Stumbling and fumbling in the dark is difficult at best and painful at worse. It depends more on memory – remembering where your glasses are or where you put your slippers – feeling around until you find them. And then, you forget the cup of water or the book that you also placed near them, overturning the water, or sending the book tumbling to the floor with a crash. Might as well turn on the light since everyone's up now!

We were never meant to be creatures of the night. We have neither the night vision of the owl nor the radar of the bat by which to navigate. Darkness was never meant to be our friend. John told us that "God is light . . . not a trace of darkness in him," and He created us to live our days in light, not forage around in the darkness of the night. Thus, "If we claim that we experience a shared life with him and continue to stumble around in the dark, we're obviously lying through our teeth – we're not living what we claim."

Sin does that, you know – makes us liars before God and men. Satan is a liar and encourages us to live the lie, believe the lie, keep up the lies we tell ourselves and others. We call it "hypocrisy" – saying one thing while doing another. Hypocrisy is off-setting to our relationships and off-putting to observers, so we practice in the shadows what we dare not do in the light of day.

"But if we walk in the light, God himself being the light, we also experience a shared life with one another, as the sacrificed blood of Jesus, God's Son, purges all our sins." While darkness falls with the setting of the sun, there's a Son who never sets, never slumbers – present and ever watchful. Jesus said of Himself, "I am the world's light. No one who follows me stumbles around in the darkness. I provide plenty of light to live in."[2]

So do yourself a favor and turn on the light; your shins and toes will thank you.

Prayer: Glorious Light of the heavens, cast the beams of Your grace upon us who walk the earthly journey, shining Your love and mercy upon us that we neither stumble nor fall in the darkness of the devil, the world, and our own sinful flesh; through You, O Jesus, the precious Light from God. Amen.

[2] John 8:12, MSG.

1 John 1:8-9, MSG

"If we claim we're free of sin, we're only fooling ourselves. A claim like that is nonsense. One the other hand, if we admit our sins - make a clean breast of them - he won't let us down; he'll be true to himself. He'll forgive our sins and purge us of all wrongdoing."

What kinds of lies do you tell yourself during the day? There can be the "Self-Lies" such as "I must be perfect," or, "I can only be happy when things go my way." We often tell ourselves the "Worldly Lies" that "Life should be fair," or, "You can have it all." We tell ourselves lies about our relationships ("You should be like me") and even accept "Religious Lies" ("God's love must be earned," and, "A good Christian doesn't feel angry or anxious or depressed"). A good lie may have an element of truth in it, but 90% true is still not truth.

One of the most insidious lies we tell ourselves is that everything is okay between God and me. John puts it this way: "If we claim we're free of sin, we're only fooling ourselves." I'll never forget hearing a fellow pastor vent, "I don't like the phrase, 'I, a poor, miserable sinner...' because I'm not a 'poor, miserable sinner.' I'm a child of God!" There's some truth in his words, for we are baptized into God's family – thus, we are His kids. But that doesn't change the fact that I'm a sinner, still. I will always be a child of man, "brought forth in iniquity, and in sin did my mother conceive me" (Psalm 51:5, ESV). In His grace, God has called, gathered, and enlightened me (per Luther); by His mercy, He has cleansed me through the sacrifice of Jesus. I am forgiven. I have been redeemed. But I'm still a sinner – and so are you – and to think otherwise? "A claim like that is nonsense."

A lie can fool people for a little while, but it notoriously fails in the long run. You can keep telling yourself things that you know aren't true, but that won't change what is. "On the other hand, if we admit our sins – make a clean breast of them – he won't let us down; he'll be true to himself. He'll forgive our sins and purge us of all wrongdoing." Better to deal with the truth than perpetuate the lie. Confessing "what was" and "what is" in your life is what gets you down the road to "what will be" on God's path laid out for you. For in stating the "what is" is to invite God to speak His truth: "Your sins are forgiven you in the name of the Father and of the Son and of the Holy Spirit. Go in peace. Amen." There's the truth for your life!

Prayer: Blessed Jesus, by Your cross and death, You brought redemption and mercy to humankind. Move us to acknowledge the truth about ourselves so that You can speak the truth of Your grace into our lives. Thank You for the mercy that declares us sinners the forgiven and beloved children of God – for that is what You declare us to be! Amen.

1 John 1:10, MSG

"If we claim that we've never sinned, we out-and-out contradict God - make a liar out of him. A claim like that only shows off our ignorance of God."

I have always loved the interchange between the politician Pilate and the accused King, Jesus: "Then Pilate said, 'So, are you a king or not?' Jesus answered, 'You tell me. Because I am King, I was born and entered the world so that I could witness to the truth. Everyone who care for truth, who has any feeling for the truth, recognizes my voice.'" And here's the part I love: "Pilate said, 'What is truth?'"[3] The politician knows he's being played by the Jews – knows this Jesus who stands before him isn't guilty of anything but stirring up the jealousy and resentment of the religious-types. He'd like to let Jesus go because He's innocent – but that's an inconvenient truth about to be sacrificed on the altar of political expedience. Truth would not win out in Jerusalem today!

"If we claim that we've never sinned, we out-and-out contradict God – make a liar out of him." The truth-be-told is often not; we don't want to see the truth of ourselves – whether before God or (one might say, especially so) before others. We'll wear the masks and put on the facades so others will think the best of us. We'll approach God with our excuses rather than our confession. We think we're good at keeping secrets, but we're not. "A claim like that only shows off our ignorance of God." The fact of the matter is that God knows us all-too-well – every pimple, every blemish, every bruise. He knows us and loves us anyway. He loved you enough to send His Son for you – and me – and, well . . . everyone! "This is how much God loved the world: He

[3] John 18:37-38, MSG.

gave his Son, his one and only Son. And this is why: so that no one need be destroyed; by believing in him, anyone can have a whole and lasting life."[4]

Truth-be-told (when it is), you and I and everyone else are all sinners – people who do not and cannot live up to God's expectations. We deserve nothing from Him, but receive, instead, His grace and mercy, His forgiveness and the promise of forever life beginning here and now. Truth-be-told, God is good even (and, especially) when we're not!

Prayer: Holy God, whose truth was made flesh and blood in Jesus and whose love made known through His redeeming sacrifice, teach us to embrace what is true about ourselves that we may receive what is true about You – unconditional love and unlimited mercy; through Your Son, Jesus, who is the Way, the Truth, and the Life. Amen.

[4] John 3:16, MSG.

1 John 2:1-2, MSG

"I write this, dear children, to guide you out of sin. But if anyone does sin, we have a Priest-Friend in the presence of the Father: Jesus Christ, righteous Christ. When he served as a sacrifice for our sins, he solved the sin problem for good - not only ours, but the whole world's."

"It's going to rain today," Mom said, "you need to take your raincoat."

"I don't want to take my raincoat, it's too balky and I don't want to have to carry it around!"

"Fine by me – but it's going to rain and you're going to get wet. Don't cry to me when you do!"

I bounded out the door and ran to the Elementary School where the bus would unload the little kids and then take us to Jr. High. I wasn't alone: no one else had raincoats. A couple of girls had umbrellas forced upon them by their mothers. They would be thankful for their mothers' insistence just as the rest of us were sorry when the downpours came after lunch! I got soaked to my bones on the run home from the bus stop! I wished I had brought my raincoat!

Waking each day, we face the realization that it's a time of sin coming our way. Though the clouds have not broken across the horizon, they're growing in intensity, building toward the climatic drenching rains. Temptation. Anger. Resentment, Anxiety. No one foresees when the rain bands arrive; but we can anticipate getting wet! We should have brought something to protect us.

"I write this, dear children, to guide you out of sin. But if anyone does sin, we have a Priest-Friend in the presence of the Father: Jesus Christ, righteous Christ." I inwardly smile at the irony – "if anyone does sin." Of course we'll sin! That's what sinners do – sin! We stand out in the downpour, soaked to the bone. But we don't have to – and that's the point: "God grants us forgiveness-assurance in His Son, "righteous Christ."

"When he served as a sacrifice for our sins, he solved the sin problem for good – not only ours, but the whole world's." Jesus paid humankind's debt to sin through His sacrifice on the cross. He laid down His life for ours. As the Priest, He sacrifices the perfect Lamb to buy our freedom from the dominion of sin, death, and hell. As the Lamb, He takes away the sins of the world.

The storm clouds are gathering again today; the devil, the world, and our own sinful flesh are about to rain down all over us. Better take your raincoat. By faith, put on Jesus – and stay dry out there!

Prayer: Father God, Your mercies are new to us each day in Jesus Christ. Prepare us to face each day, clothed in "righteous Christ," that we neither succumb or indulge in running in the rain and jumping in the puddles along our daily walk. Amen.

1 John 2:3-4, MSG

"Here's how we can be sure that we know God in the right way: Keep his commandments. If someone claims, 'I know him well!' but doesn't keep his commandments, he's obviously a liar. His life doesn't match his words."

I remember fondly what we lovingly referred to as a Lutheran campfire song, "They Will Know We Are Christians By Our Love." The song is about how we live our lives in a manner that reflects Christ. Theologians refer to this as "sanctification" or living a holy life. To "sanctify" is to make or declare something (or someone) as "holy." When we are said to be "sanctified," it means that Someone other than ourselves makes us or declares us "holy." To live a "sanctified" life is to live in such a way as to reflect the new status you have been given. Even the title "Christian" speaks to the matter of "sanctification," because the addition of the suffix "-ian" to Christ literally creates the concept of being "Christ-like," or, as Luther was fond of saying, "little Christs." We live the "sanctified," "Christ-like" life in thankfulness to Christ who "sanctified" us through His sacrifice on the cross. We don't try to turn our "sanctification" into the effort of pleasing God with our works. Forgiveness (i.e., justification) is God's gift to us – holiness (sanctification) is our response to Him. "Here's how we can be sure that we know God in the right way: Keep his commandments."

It's not easy for the unholy children of men to live lives of holiness. In fact, by our own means, it's impossible. That is why Jesus sends the Holy Spirit to us in the Word and through the Sacraments – to encourage, empower, and enable the people of God to live like the people of God. "If someone claims, 'I know him well!' but doesn't keep his commandments, he's obviously a liar. His life doesn't match his words." Will you make mistakes and potentially fail miserably? Yes, you will – just like I often do! But the key to sanctification is not about what you do, but what God has done for you in Christ and what He chooses to do through You in Jesus' name. Strive to make your life match your words!

Prayer: Holy God, Who, in Your mercy calls us "holy" by the blood of Jesus, enable us to know Your mercy despite our mistakes; empower our lives to reflect Your grace, and encourage us to "walk our talk" as Your children, to the glory of Jesus' name. Amen.

1 John 2:5-6, MSG

"But the one who keeps God's word is the person in whom we see God's mature love. This is the only way to be sure we're in God. Anyone who claims to be intimate with God ought to live the same kind of life Jesus lived."

St. John, the "beloved" and "elder," writes to Christians on how to know other Christians. False teachers had infiltrated their gatherings, teaching ideas that questioned the Gospel the believers had been taught. How do you know who's right? How do you know what to believe?

Our "Christ-ianity" is dependent upon our connection to Christ. Without being trite, if you take "Christ" out of "Christianity," you're left with an "-ianity" that will seek to connect with something else, such as "churchianity" or "lesbianity" or "sportianity." When we believe in something (or Someone) that becomes your foci and from that develops your practice; it becomes your "-ianity." "Churchianity" replaces Christ with a dedicated, albeit dysfunctional fixation on church "stuff" rather than the Lord of the Church. "Lesbianity" is defined as the formal religion of liberated lesbians while "Sportianity" is a reference to Christian athletic ministries that focus athletic achievement as the vehicle with which to honor God (you just can't make this stuff up!). Take Christ out of the equation and people will replace Him with someone or something else.

Our connection to Christ is found in our connecting to Him and His Spirit's indwelling connection to us that is found in God's Word. "But the one who keeps God's word is the person in whom we see God's mature love." When computers first burst forth on the scene, we heard an interesting phrase being circulated – "Garbage in, garbage out." It meant that a computer will only process the data given to it; insufficient or inaccurate data meant any answer would be similarly insufficient or inaccurate. What we fill ourselves with leads to how we view life. If we see everything through a lens of fear, for example, we will be perpetually frightened by most everything. If we look at life from a scientific perspective, we miss out on the mysterious aspects of life and can lack an emotional appreciation for nature that allows us to see the beauty of a butterfly without trying to figure out the laws of aerodynamics to explain how it flies. Look at life from one perspective and that will be the perspective from which you will think and act. Look at God's world through God's eyes, you come to see things from His perspective. Look at the world and people from a different perspective and you will respond differently to them, without the compassion of "God's mature love." Keeping God's Word – which requires reading, meditating on, and knowing that Word – "is the only way to be sure we're in God."

Thus, our "Christianity" is a deep and abiding connection to Christ that gives us Christ's perspective on the world, moving us to function in this world with His heart in ours. "Anyone who claims to be intimate with God ought to live the same kind of life Jesus lived." Our "Christianity" should involve our "Christlikeness" to be on display, revealing our faith and trust in Jesus to be seen and considered by others.

Prayer: Daily draw us to Your Word, O God, for there we meet Jesus; and move us to read and accept that Word that we increase in faith and devotion to Christ, demonstrating Your mature love that brings honor to You and hope to our neighbors. Amen.

1 John 2:7-8, *MSG*

"My dear friends, I'm not writing anything new here. This is the oldest commandment in the book, and you've known it from day one. It's always been implicit in the Message you've heard. On the other hand, perhaps it is new, freshly minted as it is in both Christ and you - the darkness on its way out and the True Light already blazing!"

Did you hear the story about the newly-ordained pastor's arrival at his first parish? After a beautiful ordination and installation service, the congregation anticipated his first sermon. The church was full. The young pastor stood straight and tall in the pulpit: "My text is from 1 John 4:7 – 'Beloved, let us love one another, for love is from God, and whoever loves has been born of God and knows God." Everyone was delighted in his delivery and commented favorably on his sermon. The next week, he preached the same sermon – word-for-word. While puzzled, most members thought that maybe he hadn't had time to write a new sermon while trying to settle in. But when he preached the same sermon a third Sunday in a row, tongues began wagging and people approached the elders for them to say something to the pastor. The elders decided to wait and see, but the next week, the same sermon.

So the elders approached the young pastor: "Pastor, why do you keep preaching the same sermon? It's nice and all, but we've heard it for four weeks in a row!"

The pastor replied, "I know that I've preached the same sermon four times, but nothing has changed so I figured no one was listening!"

"My dear friends, I'm not writing anything new here. This is the oldest commandment in the book, and you've known it from day one. It's always been implicit in the Message you've heard." Where the false teachers were expounding all kinds of new thoughts and teachings, John is encouraging that second generation of believers to stick with the tried-and-true Gospel they've been taught. It seems to be a part of our human nature to seek out the "new and improved" things in life. Advances are made and our lifestyles can benefit; but some of the "new" presents challenges and even dangers unforeseen in their development. When it comes to the Gospel, there is nothing new needed, even if something new is desired. The false teachers were, with their teachings, circling back to the darkness of the sinful, human condition. "On the other hand, perhaps it [the Message] is new, freshly minted as it is in both Christ and you – the darkness on its way out and the True Light already blazing!

Perhaps, we should read and hear that "old, old story" again and again since it seems that nothing really has changed!

Prayer: Father God, send the Spirit to our hearts and minds, reminding us of the truth and encouraging us to remain faithful in our hearts even as You have been faithful in Your Promises; through Jesus Christ, Your Son our Lord. Amen.

1 John 2:9-11, MSG

"Anyone who claims to live in God's light and hates a brother or sister is still in the dark. It's the person who loves brother and sister who dwells in God's light and doesn't block the light from others. But whoever hates is still in the dark, stumbles around in the dark, doesn't know which end is up, blinded by the darkness."

I have always been bemused at how we can be members of the Body of Christ but espouse acrimony, bitterness, even hatred for one another. I've been involved in my fair share of conflict – understanding that conflict is disagreement unresolved. I've tried to keep watch over my words for the sake of my relationships with the brother or sister with whom I'm dealing – after, all, we're brothers and sisters, right? But it's too easy to move from a simple disagreement to a church-wide conflict to vitriolic expressions of hatred – we're probably been there, done that – and it's usually over things that have little or no eternal consequence, such as the color of carpet or pew cushions. Why are there Second and Third churches in the same town? Usually because the First church had a nasty conflict.

The key to dealing with and overcoming conflict is recognizing the higher goal or purpose for your group. What is the "mission" or "vision" that compels us to work through our issues? What unites and motivates us to move forward . . . together? Only when we surrender our personal preferences or bias to something (or Someone) greater than ourselves will we stop our petty bickering and angry diatribes against one another. It's not all about me just like it's not all about you. For Christians, it's supposed to be all about Christ.

This is John's point: "It's the person who loves brother and sister who dwells in God's light and doesn't block the light from others." To keep hatred at bay in my relationships with others means that I need a higher purpose to guide how I act toward them – such as the cross of Jesus. There, He loved me despite my sins and failures; there, He also loved the person with whom I may be in conflict, too. "Anyone who claims to live in God's light and hates a brother or sister is still in the dark." My tribe may not be fond of the term, but I "surrender" to Christ's purpose when I come to faith in Him as Lord and Savior – a true gift from God. Led to faith by the Spirit, my faith both informs and inspires my choices moving forward – including how I deal with the people of my "sphere of influence." In my faith I choose to surrender to God's true light. "But whoever hates is still in the dark, stumbles around in the dark, doesn't know which end is up, blinded by the darkness." Saved by God's undeserved and unmerited love in Christ, I now live in such love toward others – walking in "God's light."

Prayer: Good and gracious Lord, help me to walk in Your light, stepping out of the shadows, seeing the path You set before me. As I deal with others help me see them as brothers and sisters and love them despite our differences; for You, Jesus, are the way, the truth, and the life for me and for all. Amen.

1 John 2:12, MSG

"I remind you, my dear children: Your sins are forgiven in Jesus' name. You veterans were in on the ground floor and know the One who started all this; you newcomers have won a big victory over the Evil One."

Our faith and life begin at the foot of the cross where Jesus brought His self-giving, serving-others brand of love to bear against the dominion of sin, death, and hell by sacrificing Himself for the sinful children of men. Without the cross, we would stand condemned before God's righteous judgment; with it, we're redeemed (the ransom's paid) before Him. Away from the cross we stand outside God's grace, covered in sin, shame, and guilt; by the cross we are covered by the blood of the Lamb who takes away the sins of the world. Because of the cross, we are restored to the relationship God desires to have with us in His steadfast love and faithfulness – "They will be my people, I will be their God."[5] This truth and the hope it inspires, is of first importance: "I remind you, my dear children; Your sins are forgiven."

Knowing that I am forgiven by God in His grace and mercy allows me to be at peace in my relationship with Him through Jesus. While I should always "fear" Him in terms of respecting His power to create and destroy, I'm no longer "afraid" of Him. Rather than try to appease and assuage His righteous expectations on my life, I know that Christ makes me right with God. When I try to do things on my own, I'll always be fearful that whatever I do will never be good enough before God's holiness. When, in faith, I embrace Jesus as Lord and Savior, He makes me right and helps me to live righteously before God. But it starts with Christ and His cross: "You veterans were in on the ground floor and know the One who started all this; you newcomers have won a big victory over the Evil One."

---

[5] Jeremiah 32:28, MSG.

While we stand at the foot of the cross and in the shadow of God's redeeming grace, we don't just stand there. We move, taking up that cross and following Jesus. We take the cross home with us. We take the cross to work. We take the cross into our meetings, our conversations, our friendships, knowing the victory that is ours in Jesus, sharing that hope wherever we go and in whatever we do. God sends us out in His grace to be His instruments of peace . . . and it all begins at the cross.

Prayer: Take me to the cross of Jesus, O God, that I may see again my Savior's love and know Your mercy found in His sacrifice. Loved, move me to love; forgiven, teach me to forgive. Always keep me mindful of His cross by which I am forgiven and restored; through Jesus Christ, Your Son, our Lord and Savior. Amen.

1 John 2:13-14, MSG

"And a second reminder, dear children: You know the Father from personal experience. You veterans know the One who started it all; and you newcomers - such vitality and strength! God's word is so steady in you. Your fellowship with God enables you to gain a victory over the Evil One."

I love the tag line, "We know a thing or two because we've seen a thing or two." The Farmers' Insurance commercials share some of the strangest accidents and mishaps their agents have had to cover so as to impress how versatile they are in response. To be honest, I've often answered questions regarding my ministry experience with those same words – "I know a thing or two because I've seen a thing or two."

Between two generations of believers – "veterans" and "newcomers" – John gives a second "reminder" regarding their faith: "You know the Father from personal experience." The elder apostle is writing to an audience in Ephesus hundreds of miles and decades removed from both Judea and Jesus. How could either "veteran" or "newcomer" have an experience of the Father if it's in the Person and Work of Jesus by Whom He's revealed to us? From the Message – the Gospel – the testimony of John and the others who witnessed and testified of Christ. "God's word is so steady in you. Your fellowship with God enables you to gain a victory over the Evil One." Jesus had promised to send His Holy Spirit to keep us mindful of the Message. That promised Spirit came upon the believers on Pentecost and is given to us in Baptism as we are united with Christ in both His death and resurrection (cf. Romans 6). Staying close to God's Word where His Spirit works is to experience the Father. "Live in me," Jesus encourages. "Make your home in me just as I do in you. In the same way that a branch can't bear grapes by itself but only by being joined to the vine, you can't bear fruit unless you are joined with me."[6] (John 15:4, MSG). John remembered what Jesus had said and extends the reminder to all: "Your fellowship with God enables you to gain a victory over the Evil One."

Prayer: Holy Spirit, living and dwelling within God's Word and Christ's sacraments, work within our hearts the faith that sees and hears the Father speak and of the Son's grace, that we're comforted throughout our life with God's presence around us as we learn a thing or two with You as our teacher. In Christ's name we pray. Amen.

[6] John 15:4, MSG.

1 John 2:15, MSG

"Don't love the world's ways. Don't love the world's goods. Love of the world squeezes out love for the Father."

You can only put so much stuff in your pockets before you have to find somewhere else for your stuff. At one church I served, I had a key ring with over a dozen keys, giving me access to everything in the buildings but filling my one pocket forcing me to put my car keys, house keys, and coins in the pocket on the other side. I felt off-balance and like I was waddling side-to-side as I walked. When a new phase of building was being proposed, I saw it would require another 3-4 keys on my ring, so I insisted that there be one master key to unlock everything – my pockets were wearing out from what I was already carrying!

Our capacity to love has its limits, like pockets in our jeans. There's only so much room and once it fills up, there's no room for anything (or anyone) else. While God's ability to live has limitless capacity (after all, "God *is* love"[7]), we're not God. Our capacity to love is measured; give the things in your life all the room in your heart, and there's no room for people . . . not enough room for God. "Don't love the world's ways. Don't love the world's goods. Love of the world squeezes out love for the Father."

What are some of the things in your life taking up space in your heart that you need to consider throwing out to make room for God and other people? Schedules? Commitments" Vices? What is taking up space and blocking you from loving others – from loving God? There is nothing man-made that's eternal; everything has an expiration date this side of heaven. The trinket or toy you're in "love" with today will lose its luster; the "new and improved" often replaces the "tried and true" only to be replaced

---

[7] 1 John 4:16, MSG.

by a newer and even better. The "world's ways" and the "world's goods" will pass away; God does not. His love and His presence are eternal.

So, "watcha" got in your pockets?

Prayer: Heavenly Father, our eyes feast on the stuff around us and our hearts yearn for the pleasures we think they will give us. Fill our heart with Your Spirit, ever drawing us to You in faith even as You direct us toward others in love; through the Savior Jesus. Amen.

1 John 2:16-17, MSG

"Practically everything that goes on in the world - wanting your own way, wanting everything for yourself, wanting to appear important - has nothing to do with the Father. It just isolates you from him. The world and all its wanting, wanting, wanting is on the way out - but whoever does what God wants is set for eternity."

What do people, who have "everything," want? More! That's the stereotype but it is true more often than naught. Advertisement is geared toward developing dissatisfaction with what people already possess in order to motivate them to seek something better – "new and improved." No matter what you have (according to the commercials), there is always something better "out there." No matter how much you have, there's nothing wrong with having more, right?

Contentment cannot exist in the endless assaults aimed at making we want more, different, better, etc. A wise man wrote: "Give me enough food to live on, neither too much nor too little. If I'm too full, I might get independent, saying, 'God! Who needs him?' If I'm poor I might steal and dishonor the name of my God."[8]

The problem with living a life of want is that you can never have enough – you're going to always "want." That inner wanting demands more but is never satisfied with what it acquires. Once I feel that I can sway co-workers or partners to go along with my plans, I'll want that response all the time. As I increasingly get what I want from others, I'm not going to suddenly become content – no, I'm going to expect and even demand more. Once my star "shines" and the accolades erupt, I'm going to do whatever I can to keep the spotlight on me – for as long as possible.

Eventually, however, people will "wise up" to my manipulation

[8] Proverbs 30:8-9, MSG.

and began to look for solutions that will benefit them, too. After a while, even a "sugar daddy" comes to realize that your happiness is not based on having a relationship with them, but on how much and how long he's willing to keep on giving. The fading "star" elects to prostitute themselves to keep their name and image in the public's eye. Want leads to dissatisfaction, disappointment, and discontent. Worse – it leads one astray from God.

"The world with all its wanting, wanting, wanting, is on the way out – but whoever does what God wants is set for eternity." The contentment with "neither too much nor too little" brings a sense of inner peace to a person who embraces it. When life is more than acquisition, a person can learn to value what they have rather than covet what they don't. There's no regret of what you missed out on if you stop now and appreciate everything you have. Most of all, when you strive to live with God, trusting in His provide, you can know that you will have what you need since "The Lord is my Shepherd; I shall not want."[9]

Prayer: Father God, open my eyes to see what You give rather than my hands to grab what I want, knowing that in You are found great blessings I could never create nor seize on my own; through Jesus Christ, Your precious gift to the world. Amen.

---

[9] Psalm 23:1, *The Holy Bible*, English Standard Version ®, ESV®, © 2001 by Crossway, a publishing ministry of Good News Publishers. Used by permission.

1 John 2:18, MSG

"Children, time is just about up. You heard that Antichrist is coming. Well, they're all over the place, antichrists everywhere you look. That's how we know that we're close to the end."

In the movies, there's the concept of a single lifeform that represents the dark dictator of doom called "the Antichrist." From *The Omen* to *The Vatican Tapes* to *Good Omens*, the antagonist is pictured from a young boy destined to grow into a great evil, to a dashing, debonair businessman who secretly conspires to rule the world with the righteous protagonists trying to thwart him. Such are the works of fiction, but not the testimony of the Scriptures: "You heard that Antichrist is coming. Well, they're all over the place, antichrists everywhere you look."

"Antichrist is coming" – that was the expectation; a singular, powerful, and evil individual, often portrayed sporting horns, tail, and pitchfork . . . a biblical "bogey man." But John is quick to point out that there's not just one, but many, and they're scattered all about the place. The definition of an antichrist is simply anyone that gets between me and my Savior, Jesus Christ. Those who conspire to lead people to doubt or desert Christ are antichrists. It can be individuals or institutions. Martin Luther referred to the Papacy (not necessarily any one Pope, although he was quite disappointed at the one seated in Peter's chair at the time) as an anti-Christ because he believed the term as appropriate for anyone blocking people from Christ or working against Scripture's teachings. For John it was the false teachers who were enticing believers with a "new gospel" which, of course, was no gospel at all.

The antichrists around you are both bold and brazen, subtle and sneaky – don't be looking for that pronounced antagonist people believe in. There will be a "great beast" as prophesied in

Revelation; honestly, he walks among us as he always has. His minions are the ones to watch out for because they're "everywhere you look. That's how we know that we're close to the end."

Prayer: Holy and almighty God, even as You send forth laborers into the fields with the Gospel of Christ, the Evil One sends his unholy servants to disrupt, distract, and destroy their work. But You are greater than these since Jesus has already defeated them at the cross. Strengthen us in the sure and certain hope of salvation found in Your Christ, that these antichrists hold no sway over us; for we pray in the Mighty Name of Jesus Christ. Amen.

1 John 2:19, MSG

"They left us, but they were never really with us. If they had been, they would have stuck it out with us, loyal to the end. In leaving, they showed their true colors, showed they never belonged."

We all have former friends who, for a variety of personal reasons, we no longer talk to. More times than naught, we've simply grown "apart" due to separation by time and space; other times, things were said, feelings were hurt, and an emotional wedge caused the break. I've watched over the past couple of years as friends have devolved into enemies because of social media posts. It's sad to see.

John acknowledges the loss of once-Christian believers who "left us," going on to say, "but they were never really with us." Ouch! As you hear John, you may feel an emotional "recoil" at his words and the tone of those words . . . they sound harsh . . . they seem judgmental . . . perhaps you detect a hint of bitterness. "If they had been," he continues, "they would have stuck it out with us, loyal to the end. In leaving, they showed their true colors, showed they never belonged." The words feel hurtful, but John spoke as one who had listened when Jesus was telling His parables that would also prove to be prophetic.

John's fellow apostle and evangelist, Matthew, shares two such prophetic parables in chapter 13 of his gospel account – "the Sower and the Seed"[10], and "the Wheat and the Weeds."[11]. "The Sower and the Seed" speaks of the different "soil" where the "Seed" (God's Word) falls – on the hard-packed road, among rocky ground, weeds, and good earth. Jesus pictures in this parable what we see as the hardened heart, the "quick-to-believe-and

---

[10] Matthew 13:1-9, 18-23.

[11] Matthew 13:24-30

-just-as-quick-to-turn-away" heart, the worried heart that has no room for hope, and the open heart that receives the Gospel and produces fruit. "The Wheat and the Weeds" pictures an enemy coming after a farmer who has planted his wheat, scattering weeds among the newly-sown grain. As the wheat and weeds grow up together, you can't pull up the weeds without pulling up the wheat; you have to wait until the harvest to separate them. What Jesus taught decades earlier, the elder apostle sees now: "they showed their true colors, showed they never belonged."

Even today we see once-prominent Christians – musical artists and pastors included – publicly walking away from the faith they once claimed as their own. We may regret their choice, but we can do nothing to change it. We can (and should) continue to live our faith before them, pray for them, and commit them to the grace of the Lord. Because "they left us," does not mean we longer love them. It doesn't require us to "shun" them. It means we acknowledge that they have chosen to no longer be a part of the "us" God calls people to be as His children through Christ. John simply "tells it like it is" – with a tear running down his cheek even as he pens this hard truth.

Prayer: Good and gracious God, we, too, know those once-brethren who have left the family of faith to which we belong. Where we were silent, watching them leave while saying nothing, forgive us. Where we may have inadvertently caused them to doubt or despair, convict us, and lead us to repentance and forgiveness. Where we think of them lovingly, sorry to see them go, move us to continue to pray for them and to lift them up to Your grace; through Jesus Christ, Your Son our Lord. Amen.

1 John 2:20-21, MSG

"But you belong. The Holy One anointed you, and you all know it. I haven't been writing this to tell you something you do not know, but to confirm the truth you do know, and to remind you that the truth doesn't breed lies."

How many of us remember the struggles of fitting in during Middle School? You wanted to "belong" to something – band, sports, special interest clubs. It wasn't always easy and, sometimes, you were never quite sure you were accepted or merely tolerated. You had to discover what friendships and loyalty were all about, usually by experiencing their fickleness. Bullying – both physical and verbal – had to be endured; bathrooms and hallways were potential threats. Sometimes, the more you tried to belong the worse you were at it (or, at least, felt like you were) and suffered rejection. You just wanted to belong – to be a part of the gang – accepted and loved for you who were.

"But you belong." Previously, John had addressed the issue of those who had left the faith to follow a different path. The more insecure among those who remained faithful may have wondered about their place among God's people – unsure of themselves and questioning God's love for them. Some who had left may have served as models or mentors; but now, they were gone. "Who might be next?"

"But you belong. The Holy One anointed you, and you all know it." You and I have been anointed – not by oil being poured over our head and running down like an OT king or prophet – but by the waters of Baptism in Christ. "But when the goodness and loving kindness of God our Savior appeared, he saved us, not because of works done by us in righteousness, but according to his own mercy, by the washing of regeneration and renewal by the Holy Spirit, whom he poured out on us richly through Jesus Christ our Savior, so that being justified by his grace we might become heirs according to the hope of eternal life."[12] Martin Luther also speaks to this anointing, teaching us to understand that "the Holy Spirit has called me by the Gospel, enlightened me with His gifts, sanctified and kept me in the true faith."[13] "I haven't been writing this to tell you something you don't know, but to confirm the truth you know, and to remind you the truth doesn't breed lies."

Wonder more and wander no farther – "you belong." You have God's Word on it; Christ's blood as the guarantee; the Spirit's presence in His anointing of your life. You are a child of God; be that child He calls you to be.

Prayer: Father God, don't let our doubts dissuade or disturb us in our faith, but enable them to draw us back to You that Your Word may speak, our ears hear, and our hearts believe; through Jesus Christ our Lord. Amen.

---

[12] Titus 3:4-7, ESV.

[13] *Luther's Small Catechism with Exaplanation,* "Explanation of the Third Article,"© 2017 by Concordia Publishing House, St. Louis, MO. Used by permission

1 John 2:22-23, MSG

"So who is lying here? It's the person who denies that Jesus is the Divine Christ, that's who. This is what makes an antichrist: denying the Father, denying the Son. No one who denies the Son has any part with the Father, but affirming the Son is an embrace of the Father as well."

Words mean something. The words we use convey the concepts and ideals we're trying to communicate to others. They speak as to what's in our heart and on our minds. Words share information, express opinion, and outwardly verbalize what is inwardly thought.

A creed is a statement of what one believes; "I believe" is the translation of the Latin, "credo," which defines what a creed does – it expresses beliefs. The purpose of a creed it to express the mutual belief of those who confess, "I believe…" Creeds are necessitated when confusion breaks out. They help to define the truth and anchor the community upon that truth in the face of false teachers and false narratives. "So who is lying here? It's the person who denies that Jesus is the Divine Christ, that's who." The dual nature of Jesus Christ – the ideal of His being "true God, begotten of the Father from all eternity and also true man, born of the Virgin Mary" (Luther) – has always been problematic for some. "Is He God or is He man?" "Yes," is the answer; perplexed is often the reaction.

"This is what makes an antichrist: denying the Father, denying the Son. No one who denies the Son has any part with the Father, but affirming the Son is an embrace of the Father as well." For John (and, for us who share his Gospel faith) the fundamental truth is focused on Jesus – it's all about Jesus. Get that right, and a relationship with the One, true God is opened to you; get it wrong, and you're not living in truth – you've fallen for a lie, and from such a lie you speak devil-talk: "You are of your father the devil, and your will is to do your father's desires," Jesus once said of His critics. "When [the devil] lies he speaks out of his own character, for he is a liar and the father of all lies."[14] Jesus – true God and true man – that is truth. His name is on our lips and tongues, expressing the faith and hope in our hearts.

Prayer: "Tis so sweet to trust in Jesus, | Just to take Him at His Word; | Just to rest upon His promise, | Just to know, 'Thus saith the Lord!' | Jesus, Jesus, how I trust Him! | How I've proved Him o'er and o'er; | Jesus, Jesus, precious Jesus! | Oh, for grace to trust Him more!"[15] Amen.

---

[14] John 8:44, ESV.

[15] "Tis So Sweet to Trust in Jesus," written by Glen Campbell, Tom Akers, and Bubba Smith, Public Domain.

1 John 2:24-25, MSG

"Stay with what you heard in the beginning, the original message. Let it sink into your life. If what you heard from the beginning lives deeply in you, you will live deeply in both Son and Father. This is exactly what Christ promised: eternal life, real life!"

Repetition reinforces what has been taught, providing a foundation for more learning. Get the basics down pat and then expand the knowledge base; but never forget the basics! Continuing to recite, retain, and repeat what you already know allows the mind (and the heart) to assimilate new lessons that build on rather than replaces one's knowledge base. It has been said that people who fail to learn the lessons from history are bound to repeat them. We are where we are today because of the lessons learned yesterday and the day before. While quantum physics and quantum mechanics are the newest insights, you can't get there without basic math and even elementary algebra (yes, Mr. Davis, I still remember…).

"Stay with what you heard in the beginning, the original message. Let it sink into your life." The false teachers were promoting a new knowledge (the Greek is *gnosis* from which developed the ancient heresy of *Gnosticism*) that sought to "complete" the Gospel of Jesus Christ but went in different directions. John and the others had taught this second generation of believers about the salvation of man through the grace of God in Jesus Christ. The focus of the faith and its truth centered squarely on Jesus. Anything or anyone different emerged from a different platform than the "old, old story of Jesus and His love."[16] The "old" Gospel focuses on Christ through Whom the grace of God comes with forgiveness, redemption, and hope.

[16] "I Love to Tell the Story," Katherine Hankey, Public Domain.

“If what you heard from the beginning lives deeply in you, you will live deeply in both Son and Father. This is exactly what Christ promised: eternal life, real life!” I still remind myself of the basics in life. What I’m playing golf I remind myself of head down, shoulders straight, eye on the ball, club face slightly open – going through the same steps before each shot. When I don’t I usually “flub” the shot and get myself into trouble. I still hand-write (in cursive, no less) my initial drafts the way I was taught as a youngster. I have studied and read through countless theology books, always returning to what I was taught and led to believe as a young person. The Jesus of the Bible has been (and continues to be) the Christ of my salvation – from my youth through my not-so-youthful-years, for in Him I find hope and receive the “real life” He intends me to have.

Prayer: Lord Jesus Christ, Who does not change but remains the same gracious Savior yesterday, today, and tomorrow, keep my mindful of the old, old story of You and Your love for today and the days to come. Amen.

1 John 2:26-27, MSG

"I've written to warn you about those who are trying to deceive you. But they're no match for what is embedded deeply within you - Christ's anointing, no less! You don't need any of their so-called teaching. Christ's anointing teaches you the truth on everything you need to know about yourself and him, uncontaminated by a single lie. Live deeply in what you were taught."

Before His death, resurrection, and ascension, Jesus promised His disciples that, though He would be leaving, they would not be alone: "...it is to your advantage that I go away, for if I do not go away, the Helper will not come to you. But if I go, I will send him to you."[17] Whereas Jesus came to the world to live *among* men, He sends the Holy Spirit to live *in* men – as the "anointing" of God's people. It is the Holy Spirit that speaks to me in the Scriptures, beckoning me to believe, granting me the faith that clings to Jesus and His cross.[18] It is the Holy Spirit who makes water a life-cleansing and life-giving Baptism into Christ's life, death, and resurrection.[19] It is the Spirit who empowers Christ's words in the Lord's Supper, granting us faith to receive Him who comes with "My body...My blood."[20] The gift of the Holy Spirit is the presence of the divine Helper who keeps us connected to the resurrected and ascended Jesus Christ. With the gift of the Holy Spirit, you and I are "anointed" and consecrated to God by Christ's redeeming (i.e., "buying back") sacrifice.

"I've written to warn you about those who are trying to deceive you. But they're no match for what is embedded deeply within you – Christ's anointing, no less!" The presence of the

---

17 Jjohn 16:7, ESV.

18 Ephesians 2:8-9; 1 Corinthians 12:3.

19 Titus 3:5-7.

20 1 Corinthians 10:16; 11:27,29.

Holy Spirit and His working faith in your heart and mind is the defense against deceivers and false narratives. That's why we confess, "I believe in the Holy Spirit, the holy Christian Church, the communion of saints..."[21], for He is the One "who calls, gathers, enlightens, and sanctifies" us to be that Church, that communion of saints (to borrow from Luther). "You don't need any of their so-called teaching. Christ's anointing [Holy Spirit] teaches you the truth on everything you need to know about yourself and him, uncontaminated by a single lie. Live deeply in what you were taught" which we do as we gather around God's means of grace – Word and Sacraments. You are not alone; You have the Holy Spirit as Jesus' guarantee!

Prayer: O Holy Spirit, who lives in God's means of grace, working faith and hope in the hearts and minds of God's people as Christ's anointing; fall fresh and powerfully upon me as I read God's Word, remember my Baptism into Christ, and rejoice in His presence in the Sacrament. Encourage me to live in truth, by faith, with word and by deeds that point to Christ: Who, with You and the Father are the One, true God, forever. Amen.

---

[21] Apostles' Creed, Third Article.

1 John 2:28-29, MSG

"And now, children, stay with Christ. Live deeply in Christ: Then we'll be ready for him when he appears, ready to receive him with open arms, with no cause for red-faced guilt or lame excuses when he arrives. Once you're convinced that he is right and righteous, you'll recognize that all who practice righteousness are God's children."

In other translations, the concept of "live deeply in Christ" is written "abide in Christ" (e.g., English Standard Version-ESV). Notice that John doesn't write, "live deeply *with* Christ" nor are we to "abide *with* Christ"; rather, the elder apostle specifically tells us to "live deeply *in* Christ." Note how he brings the idea around: "And now, children, stay with Christ. Live deeply in Christ. Then we'll be ready for him when he appears, ready to receive him with open arms, with no cause for red-faced guilt or lame excuses when he arrives." James the Less (Jesus' half-brother) puts it this way: "Draw near to God, and he will draw near to you."[22] Biblically, we understand that Jesus came to be *with* us in the Incarnation and for the sake of our salvation, sending His Spirit that He might *live in us* even as we, by faith, live *in* Him. As St. Paul points out to the Ephesians: "The church is Christ's body, in which he speaks and acts, by which he fills everything with his presence."[23] Living "deeply in Christ" comes from drawing near to Christ where He is to be found: the means of grace – God's Word and Sacraments.

"Once you're convinced that he is right and righteous, you'll recognize that all who practice righteousness are God's true children." The Bible is God's story: of love unlimited given to creatures undeserving through promises fulfilled though unappreciated to a cross of death for a life unending, unmerited. Again, it is Paul who

---

[22] James 4:8, ESV.

[23] Ephesians 1:23, MSG,

says that "faith comes from hearing and hearing from the word of Christ."[24] The Scriptures testify to the "right and righteous" Person and Work of Jesus Christ. Dive deeply into God's Word and the Spirit will enable you to "Live deeply in Christ."

Prayer:

Abide with me, fast falls the eventide.
The darkness deepens, Lord with me abide.
When other helpers fail and comforts flee,
Help of the helpless, O abide with me.
I need Thy presence ev'ry passing hour;
What but Thy grace can foil the tempter's pow'r?
Who like Thyself my guide and stay can be?
Through cloud and sunshine, O abide with me.
Come not in terrors, as the King of kings,
But kind and good, with healing in Thy wings.
Tears for all woes, a heart for ev'ry plea,
Come, Friend of sinners, thus abide with me.
Hold Thou Thy cross before my closing eyes;
Shine through the gloom and point me to the skies.
Heav'n's morning breaks, and earth's vain shadows flee,
In life, in death, O Lord, abide with me.[25]

---

[24] Romans 10:17, ESV.

[25] *Lutheran Service Book,* 878:1-3,6, by Henry F. Lyte (1793-1847).

1 John 3:1, MSG

"What marvelous love the Father has extended to us! Just look at it - we're called children of God! That's who we really are. But that's also why the world doesn't recognize us or take us seriously, because it has no idea who he is or what he's up to."

One of my favorite pictures is that of Jesus Christ hanging on the cross with a caption that reads: "I love you this much, and He lowered His head and died." I have always been and still am impressed that the Bible pictures the origination of love emanating from God to humankind. God's love flows from God who is love and to us; only in response to Him does our love flow in return. "This is how much God loved the world: He gave his Son, his one and only Son."[26] God's willingness to sacrifice His Son for the sinful children of men is proof of the unlimited capacity of the Divine to love the sublime. "What marvelous love the Father has extended to us! Just look at it – we're called the children of God! That's who we really are."

"We're *called* the children of God . . ." redeemed by Christ through no effort of our own . . . declared forgiven though sin-stained and sin-infected in our flesh. Truly "what marvelous love" indeed! God loves you and in Christ covers you with a cloak of righteousness – His righteousness through faith – by which you receive title and place in His holy kingdom. Child of God – called, gathered, enlightened, and sanctified by the in-dwelling and working of the Holy Spirit in God's Word and Sacrament. "That's who we really are," now – living on earth even as we will live in heaven – children on earth while (already) citizens of heaven.

"But that's also why the world doesn't recognize us or take us seriously, because it has no idea who he is or what he's up to." As

[26] John 3:16, MSG.

we live on earth, still bearing our sinful natures though saved by grace, as we live like "little Christ's" in word and deed, we can expect that not everyone's going to "get it." Some will hear and see us and be impressed enough to ask about our faith and hope; most will be no attention or just attribute it to being a "nice" person; some will actively oppose and even attempt to eliminate our witness and faith. You've been "called children of God! That's who you really are." Embrace the love of God that He lavishes on us in Christ! Be who God calls you to be and don't worry about the world who doesn't understand, "because it has no idea who he is or what he's up to."

Prayer: So often, Lord, we want to be like everyone else – popular, accepted, respected – a part of the "in-crowd." We need reminding that we already have the greatest title and honor bestowed by You – child of God; through Jesus Christ, our Savior, Lord, and Friend. Amen.

1 John 3:2-3, MSG

"But friends, that's exactly who we are: children of God. And that's only the beginning. Who knows how we'll end up What we know is that when Christ is openly revealed, we'll see him - and in seeing him, become like him. All of us who look forward to his Coming stay ready with the glistening purity of Jesus' life as a model for our own."

My wife and I have four children (and six grandchildren) who came as little packages of "adventure." When I first held each of them, I wondered what this little person would grow up to be. Would they be athlete or artist? Would they get a business or teaching degree? What would they become and do as they grow up? As they ventured out in their preschool years their personalities began to develop; in their elementary years they discovered friendships and demonstrated initial patterns of behavior in their lives. The middle school years saw the angst and awkwardness of physical and emotional maturity while their high school years saw them forming more into the people they were destined to become. As they continued to grow and learn and entered the workforce it was interesting to see what they had become. With the exception of my oldest (whom I always anticipated would rule the world) I was surprised at how each of them has turned out. They're not what I always expected, but they are whom God created them to be.

"But friends, that's exactly who we are: children of God. And that's only the beginning. Who knows how we'll end up!" Unlike human parents, cuddling their newborn child not knowing whom and what they'll grow up to be, our "Daddy God" (Abba, Father), in His divine foreknowledge knows us: "For you formed my inward parts; you knitted me together in my mother's womb. I praise you, for I am fearfully and wonderfully made."[27] While

[27] Psalm 139:13-14, ESV.

I was playing "war" in the neighborhood with my friends and with an eye toward becoming an Army officer, God was setting people, events, and experiences along my path, preparing me to be a pastor. I'm not who are what either my parents or I imagined I would become. "Who knows how we'll end up!"

Who we are, where we are, and what we become – while indiscernible at first glance to our parents – is known by God; yet even this is not the final word. "What we know is that when Christ is openly revealed, we'll see him – and in seeing him, become like him. All of us who look forward to his Coming stay ready, with the glistening purity of Jesus' life as a model for our own."

Prayer: O Lord God, from eternity, You created me to become the person that I've turned out to be and have called me Your child. Lead me to see and to come to know the Savior to the point that I reflect His glistening purity in my life, with my words, and through my deeds so that others may come to know and believe in Him as well. Amen.

1 John 3:4, MSG

"All who indulge in a sinful life are dangerously lawless, for sin is a major disruption of God's order."

My favorite coach was a good man who insisted on 110% effort, both on and off the field. "The way you practice is the way you'll play!" he would say. He ran his practices with meticulous precision: running each play until you got it right, and then he'd introduce defensive variables to make us adapt. If we started to slough off, it was, "Enthusiasm! Put some enthusiasm into it!" We knew what he was after: sustained, maximum effort in practice to create the endurance for the game; after all, "The way you practice is the way you'll play!"

Living the Christian (literally, "Christ-like") lifestyle takes constant and consistent practice: the practice of Bible reading, the practice of prayer, the practice of remembering your Baptismal identity. There's no room for ethical short-cuts or momentary moral failures if you're dedicated to the Christian ideals, you call your own. Honestly, we need a good coach to call us to task; thankfully, we have One in the Holy Spirit. He beckons us to the Word, speaks to us and for us in our prayers, reminds us that we are children of God per His decree – saved, forgiven, kept, and loved. Will we fail – will we sin? Yes, we will. On this side of heaven, perfection eludes our sinful nature; but that's no reason to keep on keeping on . . . to practice a little more, a little harder.

"All who indulge in a sinful life are dangerously lawless, for sin is a major disruption of God's order." It's not the *occasional* or *incidental sins* that John speaks of, but the sustained sin-focus of living that goes against God's will for you. If all you practice is sin's game plan, come game time, you'll play as you practiced; come God's time, you'll be judged as you elected to live. We will sin, as sinners are apt to do – even without practice – but when we turn to God for His mercy, He grants forgiveness for Christ's sake. If we get caught up in the sin-centered lifestyle, we'll turn our backs on God and suffer the consequences. "The way you practice is the way you'll play!"

Prayer: Gracious God, pour out Your Holy Spirit fresh upon us each day. Have Him encourage me with Your Word, whisper to me in my prayers, reminding me that I am Yours in Christ; then move me to live a life that points to You; through Christ Jesus, my Lord and Savior. Amen.

1 John 3:5-6, MSG

"Surely you know that Christ showed up in order to get rid of sin. There is no sin in him, and sin is not part of his program. No one who lives deeply in Christ makes a practice of sin. None of those who do practice sin have taken a good look at Christ. They've got him all backwards."

Living deeply in Christ (abiding in Him, ESV) is an everyday exercise of faith. It begins when you first wake up and wash the sleep out of your eyes. The water on your skin takes you back to your Baptism – the washing of renewal and regeneration, as St. Paul calls it. In his "Table Talks," Luther speaks of washing your face, remembering your Baptism, and tell the devil where to go, as the way he started each day. That can be a good start, but the day is just beginning.

There is the matter of breakfast. Many people believe that a good breakfast is the most important meal of the day. While satisfying your physical hunger, it's a good time to assuage your spiritual hunger by meditating on God's Word and offering up your morning prayers. The day to come will bring its share of challenges and temptations; bracing yourself in God's Word helps the Spirit encourage and enable you to live out your faith. Since "faith comes from heard, and hearing through the word of Christ."[28], we need to begin our day with Jesus; and then we need to live out that day with Him uppermost on our heart and mind.

Here's the deal: "Christ showed up in order to get rid of sin. There is no sin in him, and sin is not a part of his program." Jesus and sin are like day and night – diametrically opposed to one another. John often uses the metaphor or "light versus darkness" to differentiate between Jesus and sin. The human dilemma is the realization that we children of men are inherently sinful in

[28] Romans 10:17, ESV.

our flesh and are only made right in Christ's atonement – not by our own works. Faith receives Christ's gifts of forgiveness, hope, and peace; but it also requires daily renewing and strengthening which God's Word supplies. We need to see, acknowledge, and confess our sins, trusting that "As far as the east is from the west, so far [God] has removed our transgressions from us."[29] Then we need to "gear up" to resist sin's continued assault on our hearts and minds. "Sin is not part of [Jesus'] program. No one who lives deeply in Christ makes a practice of sin. None of those who do practice sin have taken a good look at Christ. They've got him all backwards."

Prayer: "Faithful God, whose mercies are new to us every morning, we humbly pray that You would look upon us in mercy and renew us by Your Holy Spirit. Keep safe our going out and our coming in, and let Your blessing remain with us throughout the day. Preserve us in Your righteousness, and grant us a portion in that eternal life, which is in Christ Jesus, our Lord."[30] Amen.

---

[29] Psalm 103:12, ESV.

[30] *Lutheran Service Book,* Morning Prayer, 168.

1 John 3:7-8, MSG

"So, my dear children, don't let anyone divert you from the truth. It's the person who acts right who is right, just as we see it lived out in our righteous Messiah. Those who make a practice of sin are straight from the Devil, the pioneer in the practice of sin. The Son of God entered the scene to abolish the Devil's ways."

I have an unnamed GPS unit built into my vehicle. While it is convenient to have the navigational assist, there are times I have to override "her" commands – particularly when I have to drive through Atlanta. As I approach from the south on I-85, I know that I'm heading on I-85 north all the way until I reach North Carolina and my turn toward home. While the GPS can suggest alternative routes in the case of traffic, "she" begins announcing "Recalculating!" beginning around the airport exists and all the way through Dekalb County. It's distracting. The first time I made the trip was harrowing; I thought I was getting lost though I had reviewed the map (yes, I know how to read a map) and knew I just needed to stay on I-85 heading north.

"So, my dear children, don't let anyone divert you from the truth." The false teachers were seeking to entice people to leave the Gospel-truth for their false narrative. They may have begun with the Gospel story, but at some point, they would suggest, "Let me tell you *the rest of the story*." "Recalculating!" If I listened to and followed my unnamed (and often, unloved) GPS directions, no telling where I would have traveled (because "she" tends to enjoy the scenic routes). Knowing the truth of the route by consulting the map, I didn't fall for "her" ploys – I wasn't diverted by her arguments. I stayed on the road the map said was there and where I needed to go. No "recalculating" for me!

Our "maps" for living the sanctified (made holy to be holy) lives is following Jesus as He teaches and as His kingdom lifestyle is played out among His people. "It's the person who *acts* right who is right, just as we see it lived out in our righteous Messiah. Those who make a practice of sin are straight from the Devil, the pioneer in the practice of sin. The Son of God entered the scene to abolish the Devil's ways." Following the Biblical "roadmap" is learning and applying God's "course corrections" that keep us close to Jesus, whose cross is our navigational "North Star." Our journey is enabled through the faith given us that brings and keeps us in the salvation accomplished *for* us (not *by* us) in Christ, who said of His believers: "You will recognize them by their fruits."[31]

Prayer: Traveling along our journey's path, O Lord, we are often disoriented, feeling lost, distracted by the calls that beckon us to "recalculate" our course and destination. Draw our eyes ever to the cross of Jesus that, following Him, we arrive at our destination – Your kingdom of grace and power and glory; through our Lord and Savior. Amen.

---

[31] Matthew 7:20, ESV.

1 John 3:9, MSG

"People conceived and brought into life by God don't make a practice of sin. How would they? God's seed is deep within them, making them who they are. It's not in the nature of the God-begotten to practice and parade sin."

People speak of bearing a "family resemblance," that it, they bear some genetic or hereditary connections to parents, siblings, grandparents, cousins. My genetic distinctives are short, pot-belly, burly, with a unique nose. Older people comment on how I remind them of my dad when he was my age. On my wife's side is height, brown eyes, and unique facial features – you would know her siblings the moment they stepped into the room. Our children are a mixed-bag; two more resemble my side of the family (God help them), and two resemble my wife's family (including the one with the red hair). I recall that when my father died, there were a number of mourners I had never, personally met. But each of them approached me with, "You have to be JW's son – you look just like him!"

Born again of water and the Spirit in our Baptism, sinful children of men are adopted, cleansed, and accepted as the children of the heavenly Father. He clothes us in a "robe of righteousness" made possible by the sacrifice of Jesus. The cross is our emblazoned family crest; the Lord's steadfast love and faithfulness our signet ring; the indwelling of the Holy Spirit is the DNA by which God establishes His paternal rights. When people look at us in our finery, they should be able to note the "family resemblance."

Those false teachers who were vexing the second-generation believers didn't live in accordance with the familial codes of the faith. We know that around the end of that 1st Century A.D. some had taught that flesh and matter were inherently sinful but the spiritual and the mystical were not; thus, you could sin in your body all you wanted as long as you had good thoughts in your spirit toward God. Such a life bore no "family resemblance" to God: "People conceived and brought into life by God don't make a practice of sin. How would they? God's seed is deep within them, making them who they are. It's not in the nature of the God-begotten to practice and parade sin." Those who speak and act in a godly manner are those who bear His "family's resemblance."

Prayer: Holy Father, You call, gather, enlighten, and sanctify us by the word and the presence of the Holy Spirit in our hearts, minds, and lives. Give us renewed and daily outpourings of this same Spirit that in our speech and through our actions we bear Your family resemblance; through Jesus Christ, who with You and the Holy Spirit, are our God and Father for all eternity. Amen.

1 John 3:10, MSG

"Here's how you tell the difference between God's children and the Devil's children: The one who won't practice righteous ways isn't from God, nor is the one who won't love brother or sister. A simple test."

Back in the early days of cinema, before either sound or color, the way you knew the good guys from the bad guys were the color of their hats. The good guys *always* wore white. You knew when the good guys walked into the room; while the bad guys had black hats and others wore various shades, the hero's hat was brilliantly white in comparison to all the others – no doubt who the good guy was. By the 70's and 80's, movies began to focus on the anti-hero good guy – not easily recognized and not always someone you found yourself rooting for . . . and no white hats. You had to pay close attention to the plot and character development to learn why an anti-hero was the hero.

We live more in the days of the anti-hero than we once did; it's hard to tell the good guys from the bad. You have to play close attention to the words people speak and how their actions integrate with the thoughts they convey. The anti-hero says, "I'm a peaceful man," but is brutal and relentless when forced to fight for his sense of right versus wrong. The ruthlessness of his revenge, for instance, belies his stated sentiment. The street-wise prophet would quip: "No sense talking the talk if you ain't gonna walk the walk!" St. John simply acknowledges: "A simple test."

Once you begin to question or doubt the nature of Jesus Christ, you will begin to stray from His teachings and pattern for living. If He's God who only appeared as a man, the bar is too high for anyone to ascribe to it; if He's just another human teachers, you can add His ethic to the rest as you pick-and-choose from the options that make you feel good about yourself.

"Here's how you tell the difference between God's children and the Devil's children: The one who won't practice righteous ways isn't from God, nor is the one who won't love brother or sister." John isn't speaking of a passive disobedience . . . "Oops, there I go again." When he says, "won't practice righteousness" and "won't love brother or sister," he uses active participles – intentional, ongoing, malicious activity. He's not talking about the man pushed until he pushes back; he speaks of the person who refuses to do the right thing – the man who purposely dons the black hat. "A simple test."

Prayer: Lord God, by the grace You have shown us and all men, we stand forgiven. Some have made the choice to reject both Your mercy and Your call to right-living. Encourage us, who have received both, to deny neither one, but to live as the forgiven children of God who believe and practice their faith in word and deed; to the glory of Christ Jesus. Amen.

1 John 3:11-13, MSG

"For this is the original message we heard: We should love each other. We must not be like Cain, who joined the Evil One and then killed his brother. And why did he fill him? Because he was deep in the practice of evil, while the acts of his brother were righteous. So don't be surprised, friends, when the world hates you. This has been going on a long time."

When one turns back to Genesis, chapter 4, they find the story of Cain and Abel . . . brothers . . . the sons of Adam and Eve. The distinction between them is clearly stated: "Abel was a herdsman and Cain was a farmer."[32] Cain brought his offering of produce to God while Abel brought offerings of the firstborn of his herd. The text specifically states that "God liked Abel and his offering, but Cain and his offering didn't get his approval. Cain lost his temper and went into a sulk."[33] We know that Cain goes on to murder Abel, even after God warned him about his bad attitude. From parents of insurrection comes a child of destruction. Adam and Eve fell for the Devil's temptation to "be like God." St. John writes, "We must not be like Cain, who joined the Evil One and then killed his brother. And why did he kill him? Because he was deep in the practice of evil, while the acts of his brother were righteous." Facetiously, some people quip that Cain's problem was that God didn't like Brussels Sprouts. But his real problem was his sin-problem . . . "he joined the Evil One."

St. John condenses Christ's message to "We should love each other." There are, undoubtedly, other issues that we must also address; but love for God and for others is central to God's will and way. After all, Jesus Himself said, "'Love the Lord your God with all your passion and prayer and intelligence.' This is the most

[32] Genesis 4:2, MSG.

[33] Genesis 4:4-5, MSG.

important [commandment], the first on my list. But there is a second to set alongside it: 'Love others as well as you love yourself.' These two commands are pegs; everything in God's Law and the Prophets hangs from them."[34] St. Paul beautifully explains this kind of "love" God looks for, writing that "Love never gives up. Love cares more for others than for self. Love doesn't want what it doesn't have. Love doesn't strut, doesn't have a swelled head, doesn't force itself on others, isn't always 'me first,' doesn't fly off the handle, doesn't keep score of the sins of others, doesn't revel when others grovel, takes pleasure in the flowering of truth, puts up with anything, trusts God always, always looks for the best, never looks back, but keeps going to the end."[35]

Love for God and love for others is not the way of the world. Like Cain, it is resented which often leads to an acting-out against believers. "This has been going on for a long time." But, as Grace Full said, "I would rather stand with God and be judged by the world, than stand with the world and be judged by God."[36]

Prayer: O Lord God, great Lover of our souls and Provider for our needs, pour out Your mercies new upon us each day even as You send the Spirit to refresh and renew our faith. Teach us to love so that we don't walk down the same path as Cain, though crowds call us to follow and despise us when we don't; through Jesus Christ, our Lord and Savior, we pray this and every day. Amen.

---

[34] Matthew 22:37-40, MSG.

[35] 1 Corinthians 13:4-7, MSG.

[36] Grace Full, *I Would Rather Stand with God and Be Judged by the World, Than Stand with the World and be Judged by God,* © 2019, by Grace Full.

1 John 3:14-15, MSG

"The way we know we've been transferred from death to life is that we love our brothers and sisters. Anyone who doesn't love is as good as dead. Anyone who hates a brother or sister is a murderer, and you know very well that eternal life and murder don't go together."

"Love makes the world go around" is a nice sentiment that fits nicely on t-shirts, bumper-stickers, and wall décor. The difficulty in making sentiment become reality becomes apparent when you ask, "What kind of love?" Before you complain that I'm getting too technical or theological here (but then again, what do you expect from one who strives to be a good churchman?), you have to consider what John's "love" is. In the English versions of the Bible, we translate all sorts and conditions of affections and sentiments as "love." The Greeks broke down eight varieties of love (as modern psychiatry continues to observe) and used a different word for each:

- *Eros* was the word for romantic love (from which we get "erotic");
- *Philia* was the word for affectionate or brotherly love (from which we get "filial" and "Philadelphia". . . city of brotherly love);
- *Storge* was the word for "familiar" love (i.e., friendship);
- *Mania* was the word for obsessive love (such as "manic" or Glenn Close in "Fatal Attraction");
- *Ludus* was the word for playful love (think "ludicrous");
- *Pragma* was the word for enduring love;
- *Philtautia* was the word for self-love (better known as narcissism); and,
- *Agape* which was the word for self-giving, selfless, even sacrificial love.

So, when John writes "we love our brothers and sisters," he doesn't use "philia" to denote "brotherly love," or "storge" as in "friendships"; he specifically uses "agape" or "selfless, self-giving love." That's what Christians are and do; they love out of themselves toward others – no "philatuia" allowed! "The way we know we've been transferred from death to life is that we [agape] our brothers and sisters." It is the love [agape] we receive and then share that serves as our "proof of life," so to speak: "Anyone who doesn't [agape] is as good as dead." The world is full of eroticism, lewdness, maniacs, and narcissists; it needs Christians to [agape]. That's the kind of love that, truly, makes the world go around.

Prayer: Jesus Christ, great lover of humankind, You showed us the fullness and power of love in its noblest form when, on the cross, You gave Your life in sacrifice for the world. Endue us with Your "agape," that we become truly alive toward You and one another. Amen.

1 John 3:16, MSG

"This is how we've come to understand and experience love: Christ sacrificed his life for us. This is why we ought to live sacrificially for our fellow believers, and not just be out for ourselves."

For John, and for us, all you really need to know about God is found at the cross. My tribe has always pointed to the cross as the primary source for knowing and understanding God. Martin Luther called the Catholic Church to return to the cross, to sacrifice, and to justification by grace through faith as the truth of the Christian faith. In opposition are those who promote a theology of glory that focuses more on what humankind is capable of doing than on what God has done and continues to do on our behalf. The Christian "loved" responds by his/her loving God and loving others; but this begins at the cross where we are literally loved into forgiveness and righteousness through Christ.

We are loved by God to love: "Christ sacrificed himself for us. This is what we ought to live sacrificially for our fellow believers, and not just be out for ourselves." Until (and unless) I come to the reality by faith that God loved the world and for its sake sent His one and only Son, I will not come to understand the unlimited capacity of "agape-love" which God has shown and intends us to show to others. When it comes to the truth of God, "it's all about Jesus." And, if we pay close attention, we see that Jesus was all about people – loving them, teaching them, healing them.

Jesus' earthly sojourn was not about what He was going to get out of all He did, but what He was going to give. Ultimately, He would lay down His life for everyone out of His love for "the world." The cross was not a sacrifice for some, but for all. Our faithful response to His love for us is to extend our love to the others around us "and not just be out for ourselves."

It was at His Transfiguration that a select few saw Jesus in His glory; everyone saw His Humiliation at the cross. It was His sacrifice that makes His glory known to all, especially in His resurrection and ascension into heaven to sit in His glory. Not everyone got "it" then just as not everyone gets "it" now. But if you want to know God and what He's all about, learn from Him at the cross where we "come to understand and experience love."

Prayer:

Cross of Jesus, cross of sorrow,
Where the blood of Christ was shed,
Perfect man on thee did suffer,
Perfect God on thee has bled.
Here the king of all the ages,
Throned in light ere worlds could be,
Robed in mortal flesh is dying,
Crucified by sin for me.
O mysterious condescending!
O abandonment sublime!
Very God Himself is bearing
All the sufferings of time!
Cross of Jesus, cross of sorrow,
Where the blood of Christ was shed,
Perfect man on thee did suffer,
Perfect God on thee has bled.[37]

[37] *Lutheran Service Book*, 428, by William J. Sparrow Simpson.

1 John 3:17, MSG

"If you see some brother or sister in need and have the means to do something about it but turn a cold shoulder and do nothing, what happens to God's love? It disappears. You made it disappear."

I am a survivor of the turbulent 70's with all its "catch-phrases," such as "Can you dig it?". "Dream on!", "Good night John Boy" (you'll have had to watch the "Walton's" for that), "Groovy", and "Far out!" Like them or not, the 1970's saw challenges to values and institutions that were confronted by cynicism and a liberalism of spirit. There was a sense of "radicalism" that seemed to flow out of the "Woodstock Generation" into mainstream conversation; people refused to accept the excuse, "that's just the way it is," or (to quote Walter Cronkite) "that's the way it goes!" Social norms were in upheaval, reflected by the styles and shifting attitudes. Not everything that came out of the 70's was necessarily bad, although we can hope that "big hair" doesn't make a come-back!

One of the "catch-phrases" that developed was, "Love is a verb; do it!" A challenge more than an observation, there is a truth to be found. Granted, the "love" that was being espoused by many was not the healthy or uplifting love of the Scriptures; the call for "free love" was more prominent. There were those looking at "love" between men from a humanitarian perspective as well as the Christian understanding. The church as an institution was increasingly criticized for its various hypocrisies – its failure to speak out for basic human needs and social justice, for instance. While some attempted to "morph" the Gospel into a social justice and liberation narrative, some of the criticisms hit home: "Don't preach about love if you're not going to live it out!" As a former president phrased it, "No one cares what you know until they know that you care!"[38]

John's sense of Christian living (sanctification) can be summarized by the phrase, "Loved to love." He saw the agape-love of God as something to necessarily be reflected in the words and deeds of His people – as the living embodiment of an agape-love effect. Loved by God through His grace in Jesus Christ moves believers to practice that same love in their lives as the continuation of God's unlimited love toward humankind. But what happens when it's not? "What happens to God's love? It disappears. And you made it disappear." What a terrible judgment to be pronounced upon those dependent on the love of God in Christ!

Prayer: Holy God, the Lover of our souls, send Your Holy Spirit upon us, Your people, that we be lovers from our souls to the people You place before us in life. Make us to share the love we've received with our words and by our deeds toward others, that Your love lives on in us; through Jesus Christ, Your Son our Lord. Amen.

[38] Theodore Roosevelt Quotes (n.d.). BrainyQuote.com. Retrieved June 11, 2022, from BrainyQuote.com Web site: https://www.brainyquote.com/quotes/theodore_roosevelt_140484.

1 John 3:18-19, *MSG*

"My dear children, let's not just talk about love; let's practice real love. This is the only way we'll know we're living truly, living in God's reality."

There are two ways people can sin – actively or passively. In Lutheran circles we speak of the "sins of commission" and the "sins of omission." A "sin of commission" is an intentional action on the part of a person against God's commandments, such as taking the Lord's name in vain or hurting a neighborhood out of anger. A "sin of omission" is simply not acting in accordance with God's will rather than opposing His will and acting against its demands. For example: The commandment, "You shall not murder,"[39] is actively broken (a sin of commission) when you physically assault another person but can be passively aggressed (a sin of omission) if you witness such an assault and do nothing to stop it (such as summoning help or dialing 911). Whether you actively participated or passively watched, the person is attacked and physically (and it could be emotional or psychological assault) harmed. Either by assaulting or standing by, you sin as your neighbor is harmed irrespective of God's intended will. Love for your neighbor speaks to the protection and building up of that neighbor. As Martin Luther explained: "You shall not murder. What does this mean? We should fear and love God so that we do not hurt or harm our neighbor in his body [which would be a sin of commission] but help and support him in every physical need [which, if not followed, becomes a sin of omission]."[40]

"Talk is cheap." It is one thing to speak out against injustice, poverty, and a whole host of societal ills in the world. What is

[39] Exodus 20:13.

[40] *Luther's Small Catechism with Explanation,* Explanation of the Fifth Commandment.

needed is love-in-action: "…let's not just talk about love; let's practice real love" John says. If you were to read about the history of the Early Church, you'd learn that the persecuted Christian Church grew in number exponentially even as the Roman Empire sought their demise. How? Why? The growth of the Church corresponded to those believers living out their faith and love in the face of governmental oppression and persecution. When the plague hit Rome, for instance, the government abandoned the city and left the populace to fend for themselves. Christians were the ones who stayed and ministered to and comforted the sick, the dying, and their families. From popular support for the suppression of the Christian sect by their leaders, the people shifted, arguing for tolerance of the Church which eventually led to its recognition and the adopting of the faith as the official religion of the Empire in the fourth century A.D. The Christians loved their way past the suspicions and disdain of the people by living out the faith they professed. "This is the only way we'll know we're living truly, living in God's reality." In a day of surmounting skepticism and not-so-veiled attacks on Christianity, maybe it's time for the churches and believers to "walk our talk" when it comes to living out our faith in Christ's name.

Prayer: Gracious God, in whose great love we are made anew as Your children through the righteousness of Christ; lead us in our words and by our deeds, to live in the love You've shown us at the cross of Jesus. Amen.

1 John 3:20, MSG

"It's also the way to shut down debilitating self-criticism, even when there is something to it. For God is greater than our worried hearts and knows more about us than we do ourselves."

Why do we find it so difficult to love others? If we're honest with ourselves, we know that the difficulty to love flows out of an inability to love ourselves as God loves us in His grace – to accept that we are loved . . . that God Himself chooses to love us. When loved by God we understand that He knows what He's getting in the deal – failing, floundering, faithless scoundrels who've done nothing to earn nor to deserve His deepest affections. But God loves, which flows from the fact that He Himself is love (next chapter – sorry, couldn't help jumping ahead).

I don't deserve God's love. but He chooses to love me anyway. I'm nothing special but He elects to show me His love. I'm not that great of a person but He makes me righteous before His holy judgment throne through the sacrifice of His only Son upon the cross. Want it or not, God loves me. To reject His love is to embrace Hell's fires and damnation. To receive God's love through the gift of faith is to embrace forgiveness and eternity with Him in His house of "many rooms.[41]"

This love received becomes the love we practice as His children. We hold to this undeserved and unlimited love through faith, and it changes us from the inside-out: "It's also the way to shut down debilitating self-criticism even where there is something to it." I constantly fail God with my words and by doing what I shouldn't while not doing what I should. I flounder as I trod the path laid out before me; and I'm not nearly as faithful as I either ought to be or want to be. God chooses to love me anyway.

[41] John 14:2, ESV.

"God is greater than our worried hearts and knows more about us than we do ourselves." Failing, floundering, faithless scoundrel I may be, but God elects to call me His own. No one and nothing can take that away from me – nor you!

Prayer; "Beloved," You call to me; and I hesitate, looking around to see if You're talking to me or someone else – relieved that, indeed, You are addressing me. Father, I often do not live up to Your expectations, but I'm grateful that You choose to lift me up to be with You; through Jesus Christ, Your Son and Sacrifice, our Lord and Savior. Amen.

1 John 3:21-22, MSG

"And friends, once that's taken care of and we're no longer accusing or condemning ourselves, we're bold and free before God! We're able to stretch our hands out and receive what we asked for because we're doing what he said, doing what pleases him."

Have you ever carried a burden of sin around? Perhaps you did something . . . said something . . . stole something . . . you sinned and then tried to keep it a secret or cover your tracks, but your gut twisted in knots and your spirit knew no peace. No one else may have known your wrongdoing, but the gnawing guilt within you made it feel like everyone was judging you, condemning you to the personal Hell you placed yourself into. You felt "trapped," wanting to make it all go away, secretly hoping the truth would come out just to relieve the weight from your heart. Perhaps you were found out; maybe you decided to come clean – either way, how relieved were you once guilt no longer shamed you or weighed your spirit down? Repentance and confession allow you to drop everything at the foot of the cross where Jesus speaks for you: "Father, forgive them; they don't know what they're doing (again)."[42]

Knowing God's love for us in Christ grants us peace in the midst of our personal storms. Being loved by God and knowing that you are loved by God is a game-changer: "friends, once that's taken care of and we're no longer accusing or condemning ourselves, we're bold and free before God!" Satan will still saddle-up and whisper in your ear that you're not good enough, righteous enough, holy enough for God. But that's what he does – he's the "accuser" (which is the meaning of his name, Satan). He's right, though; we're not good enough . . . on our own, that is. God

[42] Luke 23:34, ESV.

has sent His Spirit and claims us as His own, strengthening and encouraging us in our journey. Thus, "We're able to stretch our hands out and receive what we asked for because we're doing what he said, what pleases him." Let go of your guilt and shame; they're the tools Satan uses to oppress and keep you in bondage to your past. In Christ, God grants you His eternal mercies and brings rest to your sin-wearied soul. Be bold. Be free before God!

Prayer: Lord Jesus Christ, You are the Word of grace and mercy and hope made flesh-and-blood. We confess our sins and ask for forgiveness, and you grant us mercy. Help us never again to be bound to sin or its guilt and shame. Speak freedom to our souls and peace to our hearts and minds, for our hope is in You; who with the Father and the Spirit are the One, true, living, loving God of us all. Amen.

1 John 3:23-24, MSG

"Again, this is God's command; to believe in his personally named Son, Jesus Christ. He told us to love each other, in line with the original command. As we keep his command, we live deeply and surely in him, and he lives in us. And this is how we experience his deep and abiding presence in us: by the Spirit he gave us."

"It all boils down to the basics." Whether you are an athlete, soldier, businessman, laborer – there is a basic level of knowledge (some might call them the "fundamentals") that you possess and to which you constantly refer to for success. The baseball player, for example, learns early on the need to place his body behind his glove for fielding (preventing the ball from getting past him); the soldier learns to pay attention to his/her training rather than their instincts; the businessman learns when to walk away from a deal that is going sour; and the laborer knows that there is always the right tool and the right way to do things (and the dangers of not paying attention to their work).

A favorite story I'll never forget is from the life of Vince Lombardi, portrayed by Ernest Borgnine in "Legend in Granite." Lombardi was the new Head Coach for the Green Bay Packers, and the team got "tromped" badly in their first game under him. After the game, Lombardi expresses his disappointment of how poorly the players had executed the game plan and their sub-par performance. He announces that they would go back to the basics and build up from there. Taking a football, he holds it up and says, "This is a football," to which a player immediately replies, "Can you go a little slower, coach?"

Even professional athletes know that you will grow and improve your skills, but you still have to practice the basics, too!

For John (and for us) these are the "basics" of our faith: " . . . this is God's command: to believe in his personally named Son,

Jesus Christ. He told us to love each other, in line with the original command. As we keep his commands, we live deeply and surely in him, and he lives in us." It is just this simple – just this basic: believe in the Lord and Savior Jesus Christ and love one another as Jesus loved us – that's all there is, all it takes. Like most fundamentals, it's easier said than done. But wait! There's more – God knows how difficult this can be, so He sends us help: "And this is how we experience his deep and abiding presence in us: by the Spirit he gave us." We get a coach; and we get a personal trainer, too. Sweet. Let's play ball!

Prayer: Blessed Jesus, sometimes we make things more difficult than they need to be. The Lord gave us ten commandments and we've expanded them to hundreds of rules that often contradict each other. Help us return to the basics – return to You, dear Savior, and the simple life of loving God and one another that You modeled for us and have sent the Spirit to guide us as we live in Your name, to Your glory, and for the betterment of those around us. Amen.

1 John 4:1, MSG

"My dear friends, don't believe everything you hear. Carefully weigh and examine what people tell you. Not everyone who talks about God comes from God. There are a lot of lying preachers loose in the world."

There have always been false teachers with misleading narratives talking *about* God but not *of* God. As fast as apostles and evangelists began to spread the Gospel, they were followed by those whose words "sort-of, kinda" resembled the good news but with a twist of heresy here and apostasy there. Earlier, John had referred to them as "antichrists" (and he will again) for they misled the masses away from Christ even while claiming to speak for Him. On the island of Patmos exiled from Ephesus and the church he had faithfully served, the elder apostle cautions his readers, "Don't believe everything you hear."

Confusing claims and misleading messages have so corrupted social media that some platforms, such as Facebook, formed what are called "independent fact-checkers" to get a grip on the flow of bad or false information. The problem is that some of the "facts" don't always reflect the truth, only a perception of truth. Searching the internet for your information requires more work deciphering fact from fiction as one navigates competing sources of information. Just because it's online doesn't give it automatic validity.

John would suggest that just because someone stands in a pulpit talking doesn't guarantee they're not a false teacher. "Carefully weigh and examine what people tell you. Not everyone who talks about God comes from God. There are a lot of lying preacher in the world." Don't hear what John isn't saying: Not every preacher is lying, but there are those who do. How do you know – how can you tell? Compare what they say to what the Bible teaches.

Go back to what is the source, rule, and norm for the Christian faith – the Bible. Scrutiny is not an exercise of distrust as much as it should be a part of growing in the faith. Asking for more information or for clarification from your pastor is not disrespect (unless you choose to be disrespectful). As a pastor for almost forty years, I relish the opportunity to go deeper into God's Word with people when they come and ask for clarity or for more information. They are seeking to grow in faith and knowledge and are not just trying to put me on the spot.

Yes, there may be "a lot of lying preachers loose in the world," which requires us to listen carefully to what our preacher teaches; but let's also be thankful that God still sends faithful proclaimers of the true Gospel into our midst! Let's check them out and grow in the process!

Prayer: Heavenly Father, it is Your will that, as with our children, we all grow up and become mature in the faith. Encourage us to listen closely and to hear Your holy Word as it is faithfully proclaimed, confirming its truth by studying the Scriptures and holding fast to the faith as it has been passed down to us; through Jesus Christ, Your Son, our Lord. Amen.

1 John 4:2-3, MSG

"Here's how you test for the genuine Spirit of God. Everyone who confesses openly his faith in Jesus Christ - the Son of God, who came as an actual flesh-and-blood person - comes from God and belongs to God. And everyone who refuses to confess faith in Jesus has nothing in common with God. This is the spirit of antichrist that you heard was coming. Well, here it is, sooner than we thought!"

The test of faith? Do you believe Jesus Christ is who He says He is? Do you believe what the Scriptures say about Him? Or not? Sounds like over-simplification, but these questions get down to the "brass-tacks," so to speak.

The ultimate test of Christianity is found in what you make of Christ. There are those, for instance, that argue that the Jesus of the "historically-critical" Gospels is not the same as the Christ of the "church" – a mythology (they claim) developed by the Church over the centuries. Subsequently, two radically different Christs are identified – one that is Biblically identified and defined, the other redacted from the supposed mythology seen as developing around Him. Both the toleration and promotion of this "historically-correct" Jesus corresponds to the early Gnostic (saved through knowledge rather than faith) heresies of John's milieu. Regardless of their differences, heresy ultimately attacks the Biblical understanding of the "dual nature" of Jesus Christ – true God ("begotten of the Father before all worlds") and true man ("conceived by the Holy Spirit, born of the virgin Mary").[43] "Here's how you test for the genuine Spirit of God," John writes. "Everyone who confesses openly his faith in Jesus Christ – the Son of God, who came as an actual flesh-and-blood person – comes from God and belongs to God." If Jesus were not a true man, He

[43] Nicene Creed, 325 AD.

could not die as the sacrifice for the sins of humankind; if the Christ is not true God, whatever He does – on earth, at the cross, in the tomb – has no universal or lasting effect for salvation.

"And everyone who refuses to confess faith in Jesus has nothing to do with God. This is the spirit of antichrist that you heard was coming. Well, here it is, sooner than we thought!" Some faith-traditions don't like formal creeds or confessional statements, but the Church was compelled to go to the Scriptures, glean its teachings, and write them into these confessional statements to ensure believers were confessing the same, true Jesus Christ. As John submits, "the spirit of antichrist . . . [is] coming . . . sooner than we thought."

Prayer: Dearest Jesus, Son of God, and Son of Mary, hold fast Your true nature and Person before the hearts and minds of all people. Confound those who seek to confuse what the Bible says with their personal interpretations that lead elsewhere, that the Gospel be proclaimed to its fullest and the Spirit able to convict, convince, and convert skeptics, doubters, and unbelievers alike to repent and, by faith, come to You, the Lord and Savior of all. Amen.

1 John 4:4, MSG

"My dear children, you come from God and belong to God. You have already won a big victory over those false teachers, for the Spirit in you is far stronger than anything in the world."

The writer to the Hebrews[44] tells us that "The fundamental fact of existence is that this trust of God, this faith, is the firm foundation under everything that makes life worth living. It's our handle on what we can't see." When a person lives in accordance to their God-given faith, the stand firm – they stand strong in the relationship God calls them into: "My dear children, you come from God and belong to God." This hope is given as a guarantee, not as a "wish-upon-star" longing. For a Christian faith is that "firm foundation . . . that makes life worth living." Believing and trusting in the relationship into which we are called, gathered, enlightened, and sanctified by God answers our existential dilemmas.

"Where do I come from?" I am a creature and child of God, saved by grace and chosen through Christ to be His own.

"What am I here for?" I'm a called-out and sent-out disciple with love for God and love for my neighbor enabled to make a difference in the lives of others.

"Who am I?" I am created and placed into a community – a humankind with others – and as a part of the "communion of saints," the Church of all times and found in all places.

It is not an accident or "fluke" of the cosmos when it comes to my existence; it is the will and the way of God. He calls you. He gathers you. He is your confidence: "You have already won a big victory over those false teachers, for the Spirit in you is far stronger than anything in the world."

We are confident as we hold to God's promises – as we hold

---

[44] Hebrews 11:1, MSG.

fast to God's Word. From the beginning Satan – that old, evil foe – has sought to lead us to doubt and to turn away from God: "Did God actually say . . .?"[45] The false teachers would likewise muse, "Do you want to know the rest of the story?" The Judaizers claimed Paul failed to tell the Gentiles the whole story – that conversion also meant being circumcised as Jews, not just being baptized. The Gnostics argued that all material things were evil, and if Jesus had truly been human then He would've been evil; thus, they taught that He only appeared as a man (which they determined out of their deeper "knowledge" . . . *gnosis* in the Greek . . . which they felt was greater than *mere* faith). John respectively disagrees. He points his readers back to Jesus, truth God and true man as the source of our faith and confidence: "Everyone who confesses openly his faith in Jesus Christ – the Son of God, who came as an actual flesh-and-blood person – comes from God and belongs to God."[46]

Prayer: Where Satan and false teachers would tempt me to question and doubt, O God, send forth Your Spirit, by the means of grace, to call to me again and again, and to give and strengthen in me that faith which believes and trusts only in You; through Jesus Christ, Your, our Lord. Amen.

---

[45] Genesis 3:1, MSG.

[46] 1 John 4:4, MSG.

1 John 4:5-6, MSG

"These people belong to the Christ-denying world. They talk the world's language and the world eats it up. But we come from God and belong to God. Anyone who knows God understands us and listens. The person who has nothing to do with God will, of course, not listen to us. This is another test for telling the Spirit of Truth from the spirit of deception."

If you have ever traveled to a foreign country whose language you could not speak, you know what John is saying to believers, here. "They talk the world's language, and the world eats it up." The words and topics confuse us – "nonbinary," "birthing person," "critical race" – the list goes on. We hear. We try to understand. We'd like to be able to talk to people about such things, but people don't want to hear what we may have to say because they know it's going to be different . . . challenging, perhaps . . . something that is not affirming or accepting regarding what they say. "You Christians are all alike – so judgmental!" No discourse, just accusation; no proof – none needed because the believer is disparaged as being "weird."

It could be that I'd like to hear what you have to say . . . to better know you and to then be able to share with you the hope I have in Christ. But you are speaking a tongue foreign to mine, and I to yours. We speak past each other. Nothing can be accomplished without engaging one another. "These people belong to the Christ-denying world . . . But we come from God and belong to God. Anyone who knows God understands us and listens. The person who has nothing to do with God will, of course, not listen to us." We're talking; they're talking. Things are being said but the one fails to understand the other. John's conclusion? "This is another test for telling the Spirit of Truth from the spirit of deception."

Missionaries to foreign lands have to learn three things: a new language, a new culture, and a new technology. You have to learn a new language to share the Gospel with those you otherwise cannot converse. You have to ascertain the cultural challenges you face in a foreign land – a misstep can have serious repercussions. And you need to be (at least) conversant in the common technology being used to relate to those you're trying to address.

We remember, as God's people, that Christ's purpose in coming was "to find and restore the lost"[47] and that He sends us to do the same, "Just as the Father sent me, I send you."[48] Understanding myself as a "stranger in a strange land," even though I've lived here all my life, I try to learn the language, to understand (even if I cannot accept) the culture and learn how to connect with those different from me. While we "come from God and belong to God," we live in a time and place that does not believe and even opposes Him. Still, Jesus came, suffered, died, was buried, rose, and ascended for "them" as much as for me. As a "sent one," I can do nothing different – nothing less.

Prayer:

I'm but a stranger here, Heav'n is my home;
Earth is a desert drear, Heav'n is my home;
Danger and sorrows stand Round me on ev'ry hand,
Heav'n is my fatherland, Heav'n is my home.
What though the tempest rage, Heav'n is my home;
Short is my pilgrimage, Heav'n is my home;
And time's wild wintry blast Soon shall be overpast;
I shall reach home at last, Heav'n is my home.
Therefore I murmur not, Heav'n is my home;
Whate'er my earthly lot, Heav'n is my home;
And I shall surely stand There at my Lord's right hand;
Heav'n is my fatherland, Heav'n is my home![49]

---

[47] Luke 19:10, MSG.

[48] John 20:21, MSG.

[49] *Lutheran Service Book*, 748, Thomas R. Taylor (1807-1835) and Arthur S. Sullivan (1842-1900).

1 John 4:7-8, MSG

"My beloved friends, let us continue to love each other since love comes from God. Everyone who loves is born of God and experiences a relationship with God. The person who refuses to love doesn't know the first thing about God, because God is love - so you can't know him if you don't love."

While St. John the Beloved writes so much about the matter of love, he is not alone, for Jesus speaks and teaches of love through all the Gospel accounts. Why? Because much of what the sinful world passes off as "love" is but a fragmented series of clips into human emotions, affections, and even obsessions. We've spoken of this before (cf. 1 John 3:14-15); the Greek language identifies a variety of "loves" that the English clumps together in one, four-letter word. We note that John speaks and teaches of "agape" love – that self-giving, sacrificial love unconditionally given to another regardless of their condition or situation. So much of the "love" many speak of is contingent upon the other person – "I love you, because . . ." When God speaks of loving me – "agape" loving – He simply says, "I love you." Period. No if's, no because – just "I love you." When God speaks of such unconditional, unlimited, and undeserved love, He speaks from His essential character. "Love comes from God." Our capacity to likewise love directly corresponds to our relationship with Him. "Everyone who loves [agape] is born of God and experiences a relationship with God. The person who refuses to love doesn't know the first thing about God, because God is love – so you can't know him if you don't love." The corollary would also be true – "you can't truly love if you don't know God, who is love."

St. John writes to Christians in a troubling time. False teachers actively question and deny the Person of Christ, introducing preaching and practices that have drawn many away from the Gospel. The "joy" that had accompanied their faith was being replaced with doubts and maybe some anger toward their once-fellow believers. History records that violence, assault – even murder – accompanied some of the ecumenical councils convened to secure the truth of the Christian faith. Behavior one would hardly expect among supposed Christian brethren! And this is the elder apostle's point: "The person who refuses to love doesn't know the first thing about God, because God is love – so you can't know him is you don't love." The contemporary disagreements among the brethren should be approached in the spirit of "agape" – love for one another which opens the door for true collaboration and cooperation for the sake of the other.

Prayer: From You, the source of true love, O God – pour out Your Spirit to teach, remind, encourage, and admonish us, Your children, to deal with one another in such love that our disagreements never divide us, nor our debates define us into separate camps. Rather, in the spirit of "agape," the deep, sacrificial love You've shown us in Christ Jesus, move us to be conversant and to grow together in love through all that we face; through Christ our Lord. Amen.

1 John 4:9-10, *MSG*

"This is how God showed his love for us: God sent his only Son into the world so we might live through him. This is the kind of love we are talking about - not that we once upon a time loved God, but that he loved us and sent his Son as a sacrifice to clear away our sins and the damage they've done to our relationship with God."

Suppose you're at a party and you spy an individual you don't know and would like to make their acquaintance. What do you do? Stand there, gawking? Strike a pose you hope entices them to come over to you? Or do you go over to them, introduce yourself, and strike up a friendly conversation? The first two options depend on the other person taking the initiative; you hope they will want to engage with you (if they've even taken notice of you). If you really want to make a connection, you need to take the initiative and engage with them, right?

Sort of like God courting humankind . . .

Lest we forget, God created humankind from the dust of the earth, fashioned its form with His hands, and breathed life into its nostrils. The creature, however, succumbed quickly to the temptation to be "like" the Creator and soon parted company and set out on their own. God was under no obligation to chase after His creatures; but He chose to pursue them and to make them "right" once again. He took the initiative and walked across the cosmos to introduce Himself and offer a hand in greeting – a flesh-and-blood, nail-scarred hand of His only Son, Jesus Christ. "This is how God showed his love for us: God sent his only Son into the world so that we might love through him." God didn't stare us down; He didn't strike a pose and entice us over. He walked across the room – took the initiative, made the first move – and engaged us with His grace despite our sin-centeredness. "This is the kind of love we are talking about – not that we once upon a time loved

God, but that he loved us and sent his Son as a sacrifice to clear away our sins and the damage they've done to our relationship with God."

Forty-plus years ago I sat in the back of the Student Union building at the annual "slave auction" of the incoming Freshman class. I hadn't intended to go, but my roommate talked me into it; and I had just a little spending money I had ear-marked for beer, so I didn't plan to make a bid. But then I spied "her" coming up for auction. The impulse was to bid everything I had, but I maintained my composure and paid $15 – the best investment I've ever made to date. Evidently, she never realized the commitment was only for a week. Four decades, four children, and eight grandchildren later we're still together because I took the initiative, took the first step, walked across the room, and paid good money for a good woman.

God paid a little more than $15 for you and me; more than gold and silver; He paid the lifeblood of His Son upon the cross. It's not about our love for God as much as it's about His love for us!

Prayer: Loving God, who has Created us and, through Jesus Christ, Redeemed us unto Yourself, open our eyes to see Your extended hand, our hearts to hear Your call, our mind to realize Your grace, and our spirit to embrace, by faith, Your gracious invitation; through Jesus Christ, our Lord and Savior. Amen.

1 John 4:11-12, MSG

"May dear, dear friends, if God loved us like this, we certainly ought to love each other. No one has seen God, ever. But if we love one another, God dwells deeply within us, and his love becomes complete in us - perfect love!"

"What goes around comes around." When we hear or use this phrase, it's usually in a negative connotation: If someone mistreats us, we may warn them – "What goes around comes around!" We hear a report of a particularly-nasty individual receiving their come-uppance and we're satisfied . . . "What goes around comes around," right? We relish the rapid descent of the co-worker who ruthlessly ascended the corporate ladder by climbing over their fellow staff members only to fall prey to someone better suited for the job. "Karma," we may utter under our breathe. For most of us, the adage satisfies our wish for retribution when we've been wronged – "What goes around comes around" – the bad guys get their just desserts!

But what if we look at this from a more positive perspective? "What goes around comes around." Instead of whispering "Karma," what if we think in terms of "paying it forward"?

Years ago we were doing a series on being a good neighbor as the foundation for our outreach with the Gospel. One Sunday the congregation was challenged to pay the tab for the person behind them in line. The idea was that when you pulled up to the drive-through window to pay for you meal, pay for the person's meal in the car behind you. We referred to this as a "random act of kindness." One of our members was the manager of one of the fast-food stores. He reported that a couple of members had driven through, paid for their meal and for the person behind them. That next person, upon receiving word of the random act of kindness shown to them, "paid it forward" by paying for the meal of the person in the car behind them. He went on to report that the "chain" of people paying for other's meals went unbroken for the rest of the day! "What goes around" (in this case, an act of kindness) "come around."

"My dear, dear friends, if God loved us like this, we certainly ought to love each other." John is saying, in a round-about fashion, that God loved us to the point of sacrificing His Son, Jesus on the cross ("what goes around") for us, who have been loved in order that we love one another ("what comes around"). "But if we love one another, God dwells deeply within us, and his love becomes complete in us – perfect love!" What "went" around came around; the circle is complete.

Prayer: Loved by You in the greatest fashion, naturally unimaginable to our humanity, we see how far, how deeply, and how high Your grace goes to reach us. Guide and enable us to take Your love given and make it our loved that shown, that what goes around comes around by the words and deeds of our living; through the grace and power of Jesus Christ, by whose name we pray. Amen.

1 John 4:13, MSG

"This is how we know we're living steadily and deeply in him, and he in us: He's given us life from his life, from his very own Spirit."

Have you ever received a blood-transfusion – someone else's blood given to replenish yours? It was a pioneering medical researcher by the name of Dr. Charles R. Drew who discovered how to safely store plasma and whole blood for use during surgery. By storing typed-blood units in what became "blood banks," Dr. Drew made it possible for patients in surgery or seriously-injured victims to replenish their blood levels and survive procedures, surgeries, and wounds that had previously led to death. One man's blood helping to heal another man's life – what an innovation in medicine . . . what a noble concept for humankind.

"He's given us life from his life, from his very own Spirit." Paul reminds us in Romans 10:17 that "faith comes from hearing and hearing through the word of Christ."[50] The Gospel is, for us, the blood transfusion from Christ; our tainted, sin-infected blood is replaced and rejuvenated by His sacrificial blood upon the cross. It is that spiritual transformation that sets us up for eternity – connecting us to Christ for forgiveness and life. "This is how we know we're living steadily and deeply in him and he in us..." Not only do we have His word on it; we have His Spirit in us as the guarantee of our salvation!

Regular infusions are often required of folks undergoing treatment. Without the influx of whole blood or plasma, the body cannot heal as its blood supply diminishes. The steady flow of blood helps the body heal as the illness or wound is treated and the blood-loss stopped.

Regular infusions of Christ's life-blood coursing through our

---

[50] Romans 10:17, ESV.

veins enable us to resist the sin-sickness that seeks to infect and condemn us. God's Word becomes a "blood bank" where we can get the daily infusions we need; of where the Spirit resides and empowers the Word to enable faith in us. Replenished with the life-blood of Christ, our wounds are healed in His wounds even as His life becomes ours – for this side of heaven and the kingdom to come in heaven.

Prayer: Blessed Jesus, who has poured out Your blood upon the cross for all humankind, live deeply in me with Your Spirit that I may walk faithfully with You from this world to the next. Amen.

1 John 14, MSG

"Also, we've seen for ourselves and continue to state openly that the Father sent his Son as Savior of the world."

Scholars are not in total agreement as to the exact nature of the false narrative being put forward to the early church with which the "elder" John contends. John never directly calls out specific individuals or groups, but we can infer that his primary concern for people was for them to understand and believe in Jesus as the Christ, the Son of God, and Savior of the world despite what others may have said or taught. There existed a variety of religious beliefs and opinions circulating at that time.

Europe and Asia were polytheistic in their religious beliefs – they believed in many "gods" or deities of varying stature. The mythology of the Greeks and Romans are the best known of the polytheism at that time. The Jews were one of the few monotheistic ("one God") religions around at that time. They were "tolerated," though viewed with suspicion mainly because they kept to themselves. The Jews weren't interested in converting the world. The only expansion of Judaism was the result of Jewish settlements developing throughout the Empire; but they stayed in their synagogues, left everyone else alone, and obeyed the rules so they weren't considered a threat. Though many people, by First Century AD, questioned the official and sanctioned religions and their many gods and goddesses, Judaism was never presented as a viable option – what, with circumcision and other "detested" customs inherent to their beliefs and practices. But the Christian "sect" that was coming out of Judaic roots was different. Their "preachers" were often found on the streets and in the marketplaces, preaching about One God and His Son, Jesus. This was totally foreign to most folks – but it was also intriguing as these

Christians spoke of love and worked to make a difference in the lives of others.

Most of the false teachers struggled to reconcile Christianity with their long-held belief systems. They often attempted to force merger of opposing beliefs in order to reconcile them in the person's psyche. This is referred to as "syncretism." No one wants to think they had been so wrong for so long. They were, figuratively, attempting to force "square pegs" of their new-found faith into the "round holes" of their previous belief systems. But, in doing so, they were actually creating yet a different "Christ," much unlike the Person that John and the other apostles had known and of whom they preached and taught. "We've seen for ourselves," John writes, "and continue to state openly that the Father sent his Son as Savior of the world." There can be no compromise, no co-mingling of the various beliefs for those who are of Christ. He is God. He is the Son whom God sent to save the world through His suffering and sacrifice upon the cross to affect the salvation of the world. He won't fit in one of the existing slots in your belief system; you'll have to drill a new hole.

Prayer: Just as Jesus was not of the nature of the "other gods" of Rome then, neither is He a religious figure to be added to a pantheon of collected deities. He is the One – the Savior of the world – my Savior from sin, death, and hell. May I always be found in Him and faithful to You, O Lord God. Amen.

1 John 4:15, MSG

"Everyone who confesses that Jesus is God's Son participates continuously in an intimate relationship with God."

When it comes to the Trinity, too many of us carelessly rattle off, "I believe in God . . . and in His Son, Jesus Christ,,, and in the Holy Spirit." We confess the Creeds during our worship services simply because it's what you do in accordance with the liturgy (you "non-liturgical-types" don't know what you're missing). In my tribe, we're instructed in the profession of the faith that has historically been enunciated in the Apostles' Creed, though we also confess the Nicene and Athanasian Creeds (the latter, not too often). These creedal statements, based on the Scriptures, declare the nature of God as He has revealed Himself in His own Word. They were written in the face of false teaching, misunderstanding, and blatant heresy. My Lutheran tribe's commitment to both the Scriptures and these Creeds is declared by the words, "We believe, teach, and confess . . ."

John, the elder Apostle, is telling us that what we believe (and confess) has consequences – eternal consequences. It is the person who "confesses that Jesus is God's Son [that] participates continuously in an intimate relationship with God." He is quite specific: To have an "intimate relationship with God," you have to know and confess "that Jesus is God's Son." No other confession will do; nothing less is acceptable. God the Father and God the Son's essence (along with God the Holy Spirit) are so intertwined that you cannot deny one without denying the others, and *vice versa.* The Bible teaches the holy Trinity: ". . . marking them by baptism in the threefold name: Father, Son, and Holy Spirit…"[51] and, "There is one body and one Spirit – just as you were called to

[51] Matthew 20:19, MSG.

the one hope that belongs to your call – one Lord, one faith, one baptism, one God and Father of all who is over all and through all and in all."[52]

One God, three distinct Persons – an intimate relationship we may not understand, but still we confess within the Church Universal: "I believe in God, the Father Almighty . . . one Lord Jesus Christ, the only-begotten Son of God . . . begotten, not made, being of one substance with the Father, by whom all things were made . . . the Holy Spirit, the Lord and giver of life, who proceeds from the Father and the Son, who with the Father and the Son are worshiped and glorified . . ."[53] To have faith in Jesus Christ is to also be in a relationship with the Father and the Holy Spirit, "here in time and there in eternity."[54]

Prayer: O holy God – Father, Son, and Holy Spirit – we name You as You've revealed Yourself to us; we don't always understand Your nature or grasp Your identity, but, in faith, we believe and trust in You as our God. May we ever confess Jesus our Lord as Your only-begotten Son and be in true, lasting fellowship with You for all eternity; through Jesus Christ, our Savior. Amen.

---

[52] Ephesians 4:4-6, ESV.

[53] Nicene Creed, 325 AD.

[54] Martin Luther, Explanation of the Lord's Prayer, *Luther's Small Catechism with Explanation.*

1 John 4:16, MSG

"We know it so well; we've embraced it heart and soul, this love that comes from God. God is love. When we take up permanent residence in a life of love, we live in God and God lives in us."

"God is love." If you focus on those three words in this passage, you see what, for us, explains much about the Christian faith. If "God is love," that is, if He is the essence and source of true love (*agape*), it becomes easy to understand the difference between those who know God and those who don't. If "God is love," then no one can know love (fully) if they don't know God; they cannot experience the full weight of love is they have not experienced the true weight of God; they cannot produce from themselves something that comes from Someone else – something they have never known or felt or received or shared without a connection to God . . . since "God is love." Again, we're speaking of "agape"-love . . . self-giving, selfless, sacrificial love. In our humanness, such love is not possible when it is only found in God . . . the One, true God, who reveals Himself as Father-Creator, Son-Redeemer, and Holy Spirit-Comforter. The lack of such love comes from living without God – with all its subsequent pains and sorrows and horrors. John reminds his "children" that "We know it so well, we've embraced it heart and soul, this love that comes from God."

The implications of "God is love" are far-reaching. Where love is missing in our lives, our words, and deeds, God is not at the forefront of our thoughts; the lack of love suggests the absence of God. Imagine a world that lacked the presence of "love" in any of its forms – not just "agape"-love, but family, friendships – even the absence of intimacy. Sounds like "Hell," doesn't it? The absence of love – more precisely, the absence of God's presence – that *is* Hell! That's the real sting of eternal death and damnation: separation from God; God nowhere to be found! The refusal and inability to love or be loved isolates you into our own, personal purgatory until you join the chorus of tortured souls in Satan's realm.

But where we experience the God who is love? Well, that's an entirely different story! "When we take up permanent residence in a life of love, we live in God and God lives in us." A daily relationship with God through faith is more than having a passing acquaintance; it is much deeper, more intimate. "We live in God and God lives in us." What a tremendous blessing – that God would take up resident in me and invite me to dwell in Him! What do I where?

Prayer: How could You ever love someone like me, Lord? I constantly fail You; I don't live up to Your expectations; I achieve neither the holiness nor the righteousness You desire. But in Christ Jesus, You say to me, "I love you enough to send My only Son to be your Savior; I love You because I am love." I cannot comprehend it all, but I am truly thankful for I am blessed beyond all deserving even as I am loved for all eternity; through Jesus Christ, my Lord and Savior. Amen.

1 John 4:17, MSG

"This way, love has the run of the house, becomes at home and mature in us, so that we're free of worry on Judgment Day - our standing in the world is identical with Christ's."

When by faith, we embrace God, who is love, we become one with each other – He has called us to Himself, gathered us to be His own, enlightens us with His Spirit's guidance and encouragement, and sanctifies us (makes us holy) through the blood of His Son, Jesus. God is in the house – and He has prepared a place for us to stay in His mansions. Nothing and no one can ever take away this sure and certain hope from us. What freedom this can bring to a burdened heart!

We all have "lies" we have learned and have been taught during our life; "lies," such as "I have to be perfect for God to love me," or, "God's love must be earned," or, "Because I'm a Christian, God will protect me from pain and suffering." The problem with these "lies" is twofold – they twist the truth and are used by Satan to oppress one's conscience. If I fall for such "lies," I fall into the clutches of the old, evil foe who torments with doubts: "Do I understand that God told you not to eat from any tree in the garden?"[55] He slinks up and hisses, "You're not perfect and God doesn't like imperfection." He beckons to one's weary mind, "What have you done to deserve God's love?" He challenges at times of suffering and loss, "What kind of God allows pain and misery in the lives of His children?" What should be a confidence becomes uncertainty; what should be bringing peace causes distress and anguish. We become agitated and we begin to ask, "What if God . . .?" And then, out of nowhere, someone starts talking about "Judgment Day" and we panic – all because we've allowed Satan's lies to taint our thoughts.

[55] Genesis 3:2, MSG.

"Love has the run of the house, becomes at home and matures in us, so that we're free of worry on Judgment Day – our standing in the world is identical with Christ's." We remember that the Devil tried his wiles even on Jesus as He spent forty days in the wilderness. "Since you are God's Son, speak the word that will turn these stones in to loaves of bread . . . Since you are God's Son, jump . . . [Everything]] is yours – lock, stock, and barrel. Just go down on your knees and worship me, and they're yours!"[56] Jesus held firm to God's Word rather than listening to Satan's lies; subsequently, He didn't fall into the trap the Devil laid for Him. Living steadily and deeply in Christ, His love lays hold of us and our love for Him invites Him to dwell with us and in us. We cast aside the dominion of sin, death, and hell to be taken up by the Lord and Savior, Jesus Christ. We stand with Christ!

Prayer: Lord of love, giver of all good things, infuse our faith with Your Spirit's power so as to not fall prey to the wiles of the evil one, but, rather, to hold fast to You. May Your undeserved and unlimited love course through our veins so that we are free from the worries of this side of heaven knowing we are already living with You on Your side – even before we get there! Amen.

[56] Matthew 4:1-10, MSG.

1 John 4:18, MSG

"There is no room in love for fear. Well-formed loved banishes fear. Since fear is crippling, a fearful life - fear of death, fear of judgment - is one not yet fully formed in love. We, though, are going to love - love and be loved. First we were loved, now we love. He loved us first."

Early on, as the COVID-19 pandemic was beginning, a lot of well-meaning people started reciting a paraphrase of part of this verse, "True love casts out fear." I heard scores of believers and even some pastors challenge those concerned over the sickness, "You have to have faith over fear, for perfect love casts out fear!" Perhaps intended as encouragement, for many, this came off as judgmental; it seemed to suggest that their fears of this unfolding pandemic meant they weren't faithful Christians. Maybe this wasn't what was meant to be conveyed, but the damage was done. To be honest, I tried to encourage people to trust rather than to be afraid . . . encouraged them to grasp the love of God in Jesus for them as a means of hope during the "unprecedented" nature of COVID. Hopefully, people got the point John is making through I fear some may have not.

Fear becomes a tool in Satan's shed when it leads us to doubt or leads us to disbelief. The cry, "Where is God in this hour?" is answered by Christ's cries on the cross – for this and every hour. We will all face death. We do not fear dying, per se; it means the end of existence on this side of heaven and the beginning of eternal life on His side! But that does not mean that the manner of our death – "how" we die - is not something to be concerned about. I know that God has claimed me in Baptism and has sent His Holy Spirit to call and sanctify me in the Word of His truth. Still, I wear a seatbelt when I'm in a car; wear a helmet when on a motorcycle; and I wouldn't dream of jumping out of a perfectly-good-airplane without a parachute. I know that I am loved, and loved by God; I am encouraged to do whatever is needed to be done – it pushes me through my fears to complete the task at hand. The presence of fear does not signify the lack of faith. Fear is real, but God's love helps us to get past it and live the life that God's life helps us to live.

If I allow fear to dominate my thoughts and control my decisions, I soon find myself doing nothing – what my Dad would call "navel-gazing." Fear cripples me. I'm unsure of which path to take when (at least, in my own mind) either option could be dangerous (like a squirrel in the middle of the road trying to decide to stop, keep on going, or go back). As John puts it, "a fearful life – fear of death, fear of judgment – is one not yet fully formed in love." God's love is freedom from fear – a freedom that releases us from fear's dreads and worries. Whatever comes in the subsequent chapters of our life's story, the end is already written: We are loved by God into the eternity He has prepared for us. In the meantime? "We . . . are going to love – love and be loved. First we were loved, now we love. He loved us first."

Prayer: Holy God, good, gracious, kind, steadfast – the essence of perfect love – speak to me in whispers of grace even as You embrace me in Your mercy, that I weather the storms of life and the challenges of Satan without fear, knowing Your faithfulness to me; through Jesus Christ, Your Son, my Savior and Lord. Amen.

1 John 4:20-21, MSG

"If anyone boasts, 'I love God,' and goes right on hating his brother or sister, thinking nothing of it, he is a liar. If he won't love the person he can see, how can he love the God he can't see? The command we have from Christ is blunt: Loving God includes loving people. You've got to love both."

"Why can't we all just get along?" The exasperation in the council president's voice oozed with frustration and disappointment. What could have been a simple decision devolved into a "spitting contest," and he was pondering what to do next. "Why can't we love each other and seek to work things out? I just don't get it!"

"Why do you suppose Jesus had to give us a commandment to love? Face it: Love doesn't come naturally to us sinful children of men. If it did, the cross wouldn't have been His final stop on His tour-of-duty on earth! Jesus had to command us to love and then demonstrate what that looks like – what it calls for."

To be honest, I had also been taken aback by the reaction of the people involved. I'm not going to say "surprised," because I've seen such behavior more than a few times; and I'm not going to say "disappointed," either since it happens more than it should! People confess the same faith and embrace the same Lord, but disagreements lead to arguments that lead to conflict all because we make decisions about what we think will work best for us, not what works for others or what works for the group instead of a select few. When Jesus summarized God's Law, He described the second table regarding our relationships with our fellow man, "Love your neighbor as yourself." That implies that I treat others as I'd want to be treated; that I consider their wants and needs as I'd hope they would consider mine. "If anyone boasts, 'I love God,' and goes right on hating his brother or sister, thinking nothing of it, he is a liar." Strong words that open our minds to see the real problem: "If he won't love the person he can see, how can he love the God he can't see?"

When the council reconvened, I took everyone to God's Word – to this specific passage – for my devotion. After reminding everyone of God's desires regarding how His people are to love one another even as they say they love Him, we discussed the previous meeting. It took a while, but eventually the disagreement was discussed, the underlying issues of the problem were addressed, and we were able to amicably reach a group decision. It's easier to do when you listen to and adhere to God's Word: "The command we have from Christ is blunt: Loving God includes loving people. You've got to love both."

Prayer: Father God, whose love for us sinful children of men moved You to send Your Son, Jesus, as the sacrifice for our sins; teach us to love each other as You love us. For it is in loving others in Your name that we are enabled to better love You; through Jesus Christ, Your Son our Lord, who with You and the Holy Spirit are one God, now and forever. Amen.

1 John 5:1-3, MSG

"Every person who believes that Jesus is, in fact, the Messiah, is God-begotten. If we love the One who conceives the child, we'll surely love the child who was conceived. The reality test on whether or not we love God's children is this: Do we love God? Do we keep his commands? The proof that we love God comes when we keep his commandments and they are not at all troublesome."

In His famous discourse on the "Good Shepherd" (John 10), Jesus differentiates Himself over against those who would seek to rob and steal and entice away the sheep of God's flock: "I'll be explicit, then. I am the Gate for the sheep. All those others are up to no good – sheep stealers, every one of them. But the sheep didn't listen to them. I am the Gate. Anyone who goes through me will be cared for – will freely go in and out, and find pasture."[57] The mechanics of a gate are simple: You open the gate to let sheep in or out, and you close the gate to keep the sheep in and danger out. Taking the metaphor to Christ's conclusion – the sheep are God's people, the sheep pen His kingdom, and Jesus is the Gate through whom all must enter.

The elder Apostle approaches the exclusive truth of the faith regarding Jesus, with the Good Shepherd account in mind: "Every person who believes that Jesus is, in fact, the Messiah, is God-begotten." One can hear the echo of Jesus' voice: "I am the Good Shepherd. I know my own sheep and my own sheep know me. In the same way the Father knows me and I know the Father. I put the sheep before myself, sacrificing myself if necessary. You need to know that I have other sheep in addition to those in this pen. I need to gather and bring them, too. They'll also recognize my voice. Then it will be one flock, one Shepherd. This is why

---

[57] John 10:7-9, MSG.

the Father loves me: because I freely laid down my life"[58] Christ Jesus, in His "active obedience," carried out God's plan for our salvation by being the sacrificial Lamb for all humankind ("I freely laid down my life"). Faith's journey flows only in one direction – to God the Father through Jesus, His Son. "If we love the One who conceives the child, we'll surely love the child who was conceived."

If Jesus swings the Gate wide open (and, He does), could goats get into the pen? Maybe. After all, He pictures that Last Day as a time for separating the sheep from the goats, right (see Matthew 25)? "The reality test on whether or not we love God's children is this: Do we love God? Do we keep his commands? The proof that we love God comes when we keep his commandments, and they are not all that troublesome."

Can I get a "babababa"?

Prayer: "I just wanna be a sheep, babababa | I just wanna be a sheep, babababa | I pray the Lord my soul to keep | I just wanna be a sheep, babababa!"[59]

---

[58] John 10:14-17, MSG

[59] Brian M. Howard, "I Just Wanna Be a Sheep," © 1974, 2002, Mission Hills Music, www.BetterflySong.com.

1 John 5:4-5, MSG

"Every God-begotten person conquers the world's ways. The conquering power that brings the world to its knees is our faith. The person who wins out over the world's ways is simply the one who believes that Jesus is the Son of God."

What constitutes "success" for you? As a young pastor, being successful was often tied to leading a (numerically) growing church that would be a model for other churches to emulate. Sometimes success was measured in just being able to pay one's bills. As a pastor getting older and more seasoned, success was seen in the striving for church-health as opposed to church-growth; the measure of membership statistics replaced with assessment of discipleship involvement. With more experience came better financial support that allowed for savings and experiences beyond mere survival. Elder pastors begin to look past the numbers to consider the differences being made in and through the lives of others. The older and (hopefully) more mature one becomes, the metrics of success change – what was "important" or "significant" begin to lose their allure. The young pastor may seek that "happening" congregational setting and the perks that go with it; an older pastor may have "been there, done that."

I believe that maturity is not reserved for those "older and wiser." I believe that Christian maturity comes as we focus our eyes and attentions on Christ rather than on the world when we consider true "success." The old metrics of Christendom (the "4B's" of babies, butts, bucks, and buildings) all played into the world's definition of "success." I remember going to pastor conferences (once referred to as "Winkels" – a long story for another time) and being enthralled by what my fellow pastors were experiencing – new members, financial stability, new capital campaigns, building programs, and staff additions. I wanted to be like them. I wanted a shot at "success," too. And God blessed me, calling me to exciting ventures and similar experiences. But I am most thankful that He also allowed me to see that such "success" could be a facade that covered over what was profoundly important – people growing together in their shared relationship in Christ – not just numbers for the annual parochial report. At the end of the day, the "4B's" that measured "success" as a church weren't the true metrics God was looking at. In a post-Church era in which we find ourselves, we need to return to that which is ultimately important: "The conquering power that brings the world to its knees is our faith. The person who wins out over the world's ways is simply the one who believes Jesus is the Son of God."

Prayer: Patient Father, the "bright and shiny things" of this present age often draw our attention from You. Even when we think we're incorporating worldly things for sake of connecting with our neighbors as a relevant church, worldly metrics pervade, and worldly values invade and distract us. Focus our eyes and hearts and minds on Jesus Christ and let His rule in our lives become what is truly "successful" for us and for all eternity. Amen.

1 John 5:6-8, *MSG*

"Jesus - the Divine Christ! He experienced a life-giving birth and death-killing death. Not only birth from the womb, but baptismal birth of his ministry and sacrificial death. And all the while the Spirit in confirming the truth, the reality of God's presence at Jesus' baptism and crucifixion, bringing those occasions alive for us. A triple testimony: the Spirit, the Baptism, the Crucifixion. And the three in perfect agreement."

The truth about Jesus Christ – His nature and identity – is paramount for the true, Christian faith. What Jesus did as Redeemer ("buy back") is important, but the truth about His Person is what empowers His work upon the cross in its efficacy for saving humankind from sin, death, and hell. True man, Jesus died as the sacrifice for sins; true God, the Christ's sacrifice effectively saves the world. God could not die, only a human could; and a human's death could not redeem humankind. "Jesus – the Divine Christ! He experienced a life-giving birth and a death-killing death." The false teachers questioned the dual nature of Jesus Christ, demanding that He had to either be God or human, because He (in their mind) could not be both.

The false narrative that challenged the second generation of believers then still infects certain quarters of Christianity today. The premise of Robin Meyer's book, *Saving Jesus from the Church: How to Stop Worshiping Christ and Start Following Jesus*, is that the historical Jesus (a human) existed around whom the Church foisted a mythology upon Him as the Christ (deity). By separating Jesus from Christ, people fall back into the heresies of the past that St. John is confronting. Meyer's suppositions (and there are others like him) turn Jesus into a moralist-mentor while denying His role as Redeemer; it challenges the efficacy of salvation by grace through faith in Jesus Christ which is the central article of the Christian faith. Theologically speaking, what goes around seems to come around.

"A triple testimony: the Spirit, the Baptism, the Crucifixion. And the three in perfect agreement." The elder Apostle points to Jesus' physical birth and His "baptismal birth" as incarnational evidence of His real presence – His historical existence. And John points to the Spirit's testimony regarding the dual nature of Jesus Christ through His baptism and His crucifixion: "…the reality of God's presence at Jesus' baptism and crucifixion, bringing those occasions alive for us." It is an appeal to believers to believe – and through their believing, to receive the gifts of salvation and eternal life that God the Father gives us in God the Son's redemptive work.

Prayer: Heavenly Father, Almighty and Loving God, faith is Your gift that we need so desperately. False teachers with their false narratives make false teachings sound so reasonable. The truth is hard to grasp at times. But Your Spirit continues to work through Your means of grace – calling us to, gathering us in, enlightening and sanctifying us through saving faith in Jesus Christ. Thank You for all Your good gifts and hear our plea for more. Amen.

1 John 5:9-10, MSG

"If we take human testimony at face value, how much more should we be reassured when God gives testimony as he does here, testifying concerning his Son. Whoever believes in the Son of God inwardly confirms God's testimony. Whoever refuses to believe in effect calls God a liar, refusing to believe God's own testimony concerning his Son."

There have been those who have disputed the Biblical narrative – questioning the authenticity of its words and the accounts of its authors. When compared with other ancient texts unqualifiedly accepted as historical, the Scriptures have more authentication and affirmation. Succeeding generations of those who knew the authors (such as John) have declared them as true, living witnesses of Jesus Christ – the incarnate, crucified, resurrected, ascended, and living Lord. There are fewer accounts regarding Julius Caesar than Jesus Christ; yet the former is considered historical data while the latter is greeted with skepticism. The value of these human witnesses has been dismissed in some quarters via subjective suppositions placed on the Scriptures not equitably applied to other ancient writings.

"If we take human testimony at face value, how much more should we be reassured when God gives testimony . . ." We have seen how God the Father acknowledged Jesus as His Son at His baptism – "You are my Son, chosen and marked by my love, pride of my life."[60] We have heard how Jesus often spoke of God the Father in terms of their shared essence – "we are the same – Father and Son. He is in me; I am in Him."[61] At Jesus death, "the captain of the guard and those with him when they saw the earthquake and everything else that was happening were scared to death.

[60] Luke 3:22, MSG.

[61] John 10:30, MSG.

They said, 'This has to be the Son of God.'"[62] God's testimony in unequivocal "when God gives testimony as he does here, testifying concerning his Son." The apostles, filled with the Holy Spirit on Pentecost declared Jesus the crucified as the Risen Christ. Saul, eyes opened following his encounter with Jesus on the Damascus Road "immediately...proclaimed Jesus in the synagogues, saying, 'He is the Son of God.'"[63] This one truth regarding Jesus Christ is central to one's relationship with God: "Whoever believes in the Son of God inwardly confirms God's testimony. Whoever refuses to believe in effect calls God a liar, refusing to believe God's own testimony regarding his Son."

At some point a person has to believe and trust in God and His Word, or not. Pray for the Spirit's coming and encouragement; enter the place where God's Word is preached, and His sacraments shared. It is no less than Jesus' half-brother James who says succinctly: "Draw near to God and He will draw near to you."[64]

Prayer: "Blessed Lord, You have caused all Holy Scriptures to be written for our learning. Grant that we may so hear them, read, mark, learn, and inwardly digest them that, by patience and comfort of Your holy Word, we may embrace and ever hold fast the blessed hope of everlasting life; through Jesus Christ our Lord. Amen."[65]

---

[62] Matthew 27:54, MSG.

[63] Acts 9:20, ESV.

[64] James 4:8, New King James Version.

[65] *Lutheran Service Book*, Collect 148.

1 John 5:11-12, MSG

"This is the testimony in essence: God have us eternal life; the life is in his Son. So, whoever has the Son has life; whoever rejects the Son rejects life."

When playing the board game, "Monopoly," I always loved when I won a "Get-Out-of-Jail" card. Notoriously I'd land on the "Go to Jail" space or get a "Go-to-Jail" card as I was winning the game. Having that "Get-Out-of-Jail" card was comforting – I didn't worry about losing track during a winning game!

Wouldn't it be nice if such a "Get-Out-of-Jail" card existed in real life? Think of the confidence you could have, knowing that in your possession was an instrument that could set all things right. How encouraging would it be to know that whatever happens . . . whatever you face . . . whatever comes your way . . . in the end, you win!

Guess what? You do. You have a guarantee no one and nothing can take away from you: "God gave us eternal life; the life is in his Son. So, whoever has the Son, has life; whoever rejects the Son, rejects life."

Once again St. John the Beloved draws us to Jesus Christ as *the* source of life and truth. "This is the testimony in essence . . ." No matter what life on this side of heaven may bring our way, life on God's side of heaven is guaranteed because of, in, and through Jesus! Poor, miserable sinners are made saints of God by Christ. The cares of this world pale in comparison to the promises of eternity that await those who trust in the Lord; "Look! Look! God has moved into the neighborhood, making his home with men and women! They're his people, he's their God. He'll wipe away every tear from their eyes. Death is gone for good – tears gone, crying gone, pain gone – all the first order of things gone."[66] There

[66] Revelation 21:3-4, MSG.

is (truly) a Light at the end of your tunnel – a "Get-Out-of-Hell" card in your possession.

Armed with the "Get-Out-of-Jail" card, I would play the "Monopoly" game more aggressively. I didn't worry about that one, bad roll of the dice that could get me into trouble; no fear of being thwarted in my endeavor. I could roll the dice, move my "car" (I was always the car), buy land, build houses and hotels, and eventually rule the world (cue the theme from "Pinky and the Brain")!

In real life, knowing the guarantee of forever, glorious life through Jesus, I don't give into the fears that often freeze people in their tracks. I know whatever I face in life, I don't face alone. I have another life . . . a better life . . . an eternal life to come because of Jesus Christ!

Prayer: "Blessed assurance, Jesus is mine, Oh, what a foretaste of glory divine! Heir of salvation, purchase of God, Born of His Spirit, washed in His blood. This is my story, this is my song, Praising my Savior all the day long. This is my story, this is my song, Praising my Savior all the day long!"[67]

[67] "Blessed Assurance," by Fanny Crosby, Public Domain.

1 John 5:13-15, MSG

"My purpose in writing is simply this: that you who believe in God's Son will know beyond the shadow of a doubt that you have eternal life, the reality and not the illusion. And how bold and free we then become in his presence, freely asking according to his will, sure that he's listening. And if we're confident that he's listening, we know that what we've asked for is as good as ours."

A recent article I read stated that there are over 180 denominations currently in North America. The writer went on to say that all of these denominations claim they are based in Biblical teachings and were derived out of theological controversies. If every one of these denominations are based on Biblical truth, shouldn't there only be one church? But, as previous mentioned, there are over 180. How's that possible? From a theologian's perspective, the problem is over the minute teachings of Christianity, not the core message. It would seem to me if people were to first agree regarding the Person and Work of Jesus Christ, they should be able to sort everything else out, right? But the Romanists insist on the need for faith and prescribed works for a person to be saved while the Holiness churches demand the presence of visible, discernable spiritual gifts to be displayed; Calvinists insist on a "double predestination" that is not found in the Bible, and classical Methodism argues for a "progressive sanctification" in the life of a believer rather a holiness of living that proceeds from the gift of forgiveness and salvation. Even in the Lutheran tribes we see arguments over the efficacy of the Scriptures (is it God's Word, or does the Bible merely contain God's Word – and who makes that determination?), the exclusive salvific gift of justification versus the narrative of liberation theology, or the matters of gender and sexuality.

Now, in the days of St. John, there were no denominations, but there were differences in understanding the teachings of the

Scriptures. As we have repeatedly noted, the central issue of dispute rested on the Person and Work of Christ. The elder Apostle has always come back to the necessity of believing in Jesus Christ, true God, and true man, as the Savior of the world. What part of this do we not get? "My purpose in writing is simply this: that you who believe in God's Son will know beyond the shadow of a doubt that you have eternal life, the reality and not the illusion." Here's the Beloved's hope for his "children" – know Jesus as your only Savior and have true, eternal life that is to be experienced already on this side of heaven: "And how bold and free we then become in his presence, freely asking according to his will, sure that he's listening. And if we're confident that he's listening, we know that what we've asked for us is as good as ours." In other words, don't fall for "sham suppositions" based on feelings or another's interpretations: you cannot save yourself; you cannot cooperate with God's grace, you cannot determine your eternal destiny on your own terms or by your actions. It is only by faith in Jesus Christ by which you can be saved: "For by grace you have been saved through faith. And this is not your own doing; it is the gift of God, not a result of works, so that no one may boast."[68]. From beginning to end, "it's all about Jesus!"

To be honest, some of the varying traditions in Christianity came out of conscientious concerns that people felt were not adequately being taught or practiced as they should. Disagreements arose as opponents argued for their viewpoint over the views of others rather than everyone submitting to a set confession of the faith. Off-shoots bore new branches and as the limbs continued to multiply, they less and less resembled the root and trunk from which they sprouted. Love for God and one another became a contest – "I love Jesus yes I do; I love Jesus, more than you!" Hardly the central truth of the Christian faith – "that you who believe in God's Son will know beyond the shadow of a doubt that you have eternal life..." May God forgive us all our folly!

[68] Ephesians 2:8-9, ESV.

Prayer: Though in our various circles we confess a "one true Christian and apostolic Church," we know that such a thing is not found on the earth, but only in the hearts of men who believe and trust in Jesus Christ as Savior and Lord. Lead us, who believe, to seek one another out and to work beyond our differences to make known Your kingdom, both in this world and the next. The kingdom of Your Son, our Savior Jesus. Amen.

1 John 5:16-17, MSG

"For instance, if we see a Christian believer sinning (clearly I'm not talking about those who make a practice of sin in a way that is 'fatal,' leading to death), we ask for God's help and he gladly gives it, gives life to the sinner whose sin is not fatal. There is such a thing as a fatal sin, and I'm not urging you to pray about that. Everything we do wrong is sin, but not all sin is fatal."

I remember listening in on a conversation as a kid that was a "head-scratcher" for me. A couple of classmates were categorizing sins by color. They spoke of "white lies" versus lies of various colors; of sins that crossed an imaginary "red zone" while others in the "yellow" or "green" zones. Listening in, it sounded as if they were suggesting that some sins were allowable (almost acceptable) while others were deplorable. In my house, my parents spoke of sin in only one way – "don't do it" – and, if you sinned, you were to ask God for forgiveness. Every Sunday we were to confess our sins in general, praying God would forgive each and every one – even the ones we didn't remember. That is very much what the elder Apostle is saying: "if we see a Christian believer sinning . . . we ask for God's help and he gladly gives it, gives life to the sinner whose sin is not fatal." We are conceived and born sinful children of men . . . sinners . . . people who sin and who need God's help and mercy, which He freely gives us in Jesus Christ. We turn back to God (repent), confess our sins, and hear His word of forgiveness . . . "we ask for God's help and he freely gives it."

But what about this "fatal sin" John speaks of? ". . . clearly I'm not talking about those who make a practice of sin in a way that is 'fatal,' leading to death . . . There is such a thing as a fatal sin . . . but not all sin is fatal." Are we back to that childhood discussion I was listening to? Those of the Roman Catholic tribe speak of "the seven deadly sins" (pride, greed, lust, envy, gluttony, wrath, and sloth) as those which inspire more sins in a person's life. Yet, that smacks of an arbitrary hierarchy of sin – not necessarily a Biblical one. Paul says in Romans 6:23 that the wages of sin is death – not certain sins, but sin . . . period. Jesus only speaks of the "unpardonable" sin when He redresses the religious-types: "But if you persist in your slanders against God's Holy Spirit, you are repudiating the very One who forgives, sawing off the branch on which you are sitting, severing by your own perversity all connection with One who forgives."[69] Unbelief, then, is the identified, deadly sin . . . "There is such a thing as a fatal sin."

We can (and should) take comfort that though we're often true to our sinful nature, God is steadfast in His love and mercy. After all, "everything we do wrong is sin, but not all sin is fatal." If you can confess it God will forgive it – you have the cross of Christ as the guarantee.

Prayer: Holy God, I know that I sin; I do the evil You forbid and don't do the good You command. I acknowledge my sin and pray Your forgiveness of my sins through the cross of Your only-begotten Son, Jesus Christ. Pour out Your Holy Spirit upon me that loved, I love others and forgiven, I forgive; to the glory of Your name and the betterment of my neighbor. Amen.

---

[69] Mark 3:28-29, MSG.

1 John 5:18-19, *MSG*

"We know that none of the God-begotten makes a practice of sin - fatal sin. The God-begotten are also God-protected. The Evil One can't lay a hand on them. We know that we are held firm by God; it's only the people of the world who continue in the grip of the Evil One."

People are conceived, born, and live in sin; that is the sinful nature with which we were cursed, courtesy of our first parents' desire to "be like God" (Genesis 3). Original sin is as much of our DNA as height, hair color, and other genetic dispositions. Subsequently, we sin daily and must turn to God's grace in Christ Jesus for forgiveness and reassurance. Does that mean, somehow, we're not "God-begotten"? No – that's not what John is addressing: "it's only the people of the world who continue in the grip of the Evil One."

The key to understanding is hearing what John *is saying*: "we know that none of the God-begotten *makes a practice* of sin – fatal sin." We all sin. We daily sin. All of us have a "signature sin" or two that we easily succumb to. [A "signature sin" is one that if there were a list of all sins, there would be a particular sin we'd sign our name to – such as greed, envy, lust, etc.] John addresses the "practice of sin – fatal sin." He's talking about people who continue to sin even though they know it is sin they're committing. Such a "practice of sin" dominates their thinking and rules their hearts. There develops an unhealthy compulsion that drives thoughts and actions in directions and pathways that are painful and destructive: the porn-addiction that leads to marital dissatisfaction; the overt materialism that denies contentment and disregards the needs of others – even family; the envy of others' position or prestige that stokes the flames of jealousy and rage. This is life "in the grip of the Evil One."

What is central to John's argument is the encouragement to walk in the grace of God rather than in "the grip of the Evil One." John's reasoning is simple: "The God-begotten are God-protected. The Evil One can't lay a hand on them. We know that we are held firm by God..." The confidence of our faith rests on believing what God says and trusting Him to do what He has promised. We know His commitment to our salvation by the cross of His Son. In our baptism, our new life is confirmed: "We know that our old self was crucified with him [Jesus] in order that the body of sin might be brought to nothing; so that we would no longer be enslaved to sin."[70] "God-begotten" by our baptism into Christ, we are "God-protected" by our heavenly Father until life everlasting. "The Evil One cannot lay a hand on [us]."

Prayer: Steadfast in Your righteousness and faithful in Your love, O Lord, give to us the confidence we need to trust in Your grace and providence, that we may never fall into the grip of the Evil One; through Jesus Christ, we pray. Amen.

[70] Romans 6:6, ESV.

1 John 5:20-21, MSG

"And we know that the Son of God came so we would recognize and understand the truth of God - what a gift! - and we are living in the Truth itself, in God's Son, Jesus Christ. This Jesus is both True God and Real Life. Dear children, be on guard against all clever facsimiles."

"Just like the real thing!" Not! Growing up I enjoyed sweets – immensely enjoyed sweets! There was always candy in the bowl, cookies in the jar, pastries in the pantry, and Blue Bell in the freezer. In particular, I loved good, milk chocolate. Later in life I became a diabetic (go figure, right?) and the sweets I had always enjoyed were *verboten*. I tried some of the "sugar-free" alternatives, often advertised as tasting like the original recipes. But they didn't. I've yet to discover a "sugar-free" milk chocolate that tastes like real milk chocolate, so I go without.

In his book, *Will the Real Jesus Please Stand Up*, Matthew Richard examines 12 false Christs perpetuated by modern preachers. He speaks of many poor notions that have evolved from either focusing on a single aspect of Christ or from the imposition of presumption on the part of the misguided. Cheerleader Jesus? Really? For too many, a sad commentary on the inability and unwillingness (or, just plain laziness) of people to search the Scriptures for themselves rather than blindly following shallow charlatans as they peddle their snake oil and less-than-original remedies to the world's problems. "And we know that the Son of God came so we could recognize and understand the truth of God – what a gift!"

Living in a faith relationship with Jesus Christ means "we are living in the Truth itself, God's Son, Jesus Christ." This is the Messiah and Good News of God that John focused his and his "children's" eyes upon: "This Jesus is both True God and Real

Life." There is no new-and-improved Jesus, despite the books and presentations claiming new revelations or new evidence. "Dear children, be on guard against all clever facsimiles."

I still haven't found any "sugar-free" anything as good as the original sweets I enjoyed in my youth – but then, a lot of things in life are not as good as I seem to remember them. I thank God for the original and one-and-only Lord and Savior, Jesus Christ. Anyone or anything else just pales in comparison. I thank God that John's words were guided by the Holy Spirit and convey the thoughts of God "so we could recognize and understand the truth of God – what a gift!"

Prayer:

"Thy strong Word bespeaks us righteous;
Bright with Thine own holiness.
Glorious now we press toward glory,
And our lives our hopes confess.
Alleluia! Alleluia! Praise to Thee who light dost send!
Alleluia! Alleluia! Alleluia without end!
From the cross Thy wisdom shining
Breaketh forth in conqu'ring might;
From the cross forever beameth
All Thy bright redeeming light.
Alleluia! Alleluia! Praise to Thee who light dost send!
Alleluia! Alleluia! Alleluia without end!"[71]

[71] *Lutheran Service Book*, 578:3,4 by Martin Franzmann, © 1969 by Concordia Publishing House.

2 John 1-2, MSG

"My dear congregation, I, your pastor, love you in very truth. And I'm not alone - everyone who knows the Truth that has taken up permanent residence in us loves you."

As John pens yet another letter to the church, "my dear congregation," he shifts his tone from God's love and truth in Jesus Christ, to the love he has for his fellow believers. "I, your pastor, love you in truth." It must have been difficult for the elder Apostle, exiled on Patmos, separated from his church, only able to send and receive letters, knowing that his "congregation" was dealing with opposition and apostasy – and he was stuck on a Roman prison island! His was a deep and abiding love for those he served. John was in exile and was worried and concerned for his congregation. Meanwhile there were many in the church who longed for their pastor, who had been forcibly removed by the Romans.

What a wonderful experience when pastor and congregation have such a deep and abiding love for one another! There are such stories. Unfortunately, we hear the other ones – the running battles between the shepherd and his flock; stories of pastoral misconduct, on the one hand, and piranha-parishes who consume their pastors on the other; of pastors disparaging their people while members thinking and acting most dishonorably toward their pastor. When we hear such stories, it makes us ask the question: "Where is the 'love…in very truth' of which John writes?" There are churches and pastors who have deep, loving relationships to be sure; it's just that we don't hear and read about them in the news or in the community chatter.

In my Lutheran tribe, we understand why such unhealthy relationships develop in the "bride of Christ." We speak of the "visible church," which are the local congregations where people gather together, and of the "invisible Church," or the "Universal Church" that is made up of only those people who truly believe. In a "visible church," believers do gather together around the means of grace, but they are often joined with hypocrites who neither believe nor live in the Truth. Their presence can be used by Satan to sow the seeds of discord and discontent that go on to foment upset and unhealthy ways of dealing with each other as brothers and sisters in Christ. In the "visible church," disagreements and conflict can burden the fellowship; in the "invisible Church," it is the Truth and Love of Jesus Christ which unites believers in the "one Christian and apostolic Church." This is what John is describing as "everyone who knows the Truth that has taken up permanent residence in us..."

Do you want the kind of relationship that John describes, here? Pray for your pastor. Love your pastor. Encourage your pastor. He, in return, will joyfully minister in your midst and together – pastor and people – you will share and know the love and the peace that come only through the Truth of God – Jesus Christ, His Son, our Lord and Savior!

Prayer: Gracious God and loving Father, pour out upon Your people – Your Church – the unity, love, and mutual consolation of the saints that builds us up into a mighty movement of grace for the sake of Your glory and the blessing of the children of men; through Jesus Christ, who is Truth and love in perfection. Amen.

2 John 3, MSG

"Let grace, mercy, and peace be with us in truth and love from God the Father and from Jesus Christ, Son of the Father!"

There were bumper-stickers and billboards that read: "Know Jesus, know peace; No Jesus, no peace." I like "bumper-sticker-theology" because if it can fit on a bumper-sticker, I will tend to remember it. Another one goes like this: "God said it. I believe it. That settles it." It speaks to the efficacy of the Scriptures. Gritty. To the point. Memorable. Of course, this is from a man whose memorization of the Scriptures in confined to such verses as "Jesus wept." When I work with congregations to clarify their mission as God's church, the Mission Statement that results from the effort has to fit on a bumper-sticker; clear, precise, short, and likely to be remembered by all the members. If people can't recall the Mission Statement, they most likely will not remember the purpose for their congregation – the answer to the question, "What is God up to among us?" Keep it short. Keep it simple. Make it memorable.

John's words, "Let grace, mercy, and peace be with us in truth and love from God the Father and from Jesus Christ," state the fundamental hope of John for his "dear congregation." Having expressed his love for the church, he points them (again) to the "truth and love from God…and…Jesus Christ…" For it is from this truth and love that the church experiences "grace, mercy, and peace." God's "grace" is His unconditional, undeserved, and unlimited love that He shows humankind in and through His Son, our Savior Jesus Christ. One might say, "Know Jesus, know grace." God's "mercy" is found in His forgiveness of our sins through the cross of Christ: We call this "redemption," or God's buying us out from the dominion of sin, death, and hell through the shed blood of His only-begotten Son. One could rightly say, "No Jesus, no mercy." God's peace is twofold; by our redemption, we have peace with God, and by the indwelling of the Holy Spirit – the seal and guarantee of our salvation[72] – we experience the peace of God on this side of heaven. One might want to create a new bumper sticker: "Grace. Mercy. Peace. Jesus." Short. Simple. Memorable. But most importantly, True!

Prayer: Father, Son, and Holy Spirit – as You, O God, reveal Yourself to us, we call You by Your name. Keep us ever near to Your grace and mercy that we may be filled with Your peace in the face of anxiety, challenge, and even threats we face on this side of heaven until You come to take us to Your side of heaven; through Jesus Christ, our Lord and Savior. Amen.

---

[72] 1 John 5:6, MSG.

2 John 4, MSG

"I can't tell you how happy I am to learn that many members of your congregation are diligent in living out the Truth, exactly as commanded by the Father."

Diligence . . . "a careful and persistent work or effort" (Google); "steady, earnest, and energetic effort; devoted and painstaking work and application to accomplish an undertaking" (Merriam-Webster). Pastor and elder-Apostle John acknowledges the good news that has come out of Ephesus; while false teachers and false narratives have infested the congregation, "many members of your congregation are diligent in living out the Truth..." Let's not miss the point here: While knowing the Truth is important – especially in the face of those who don't – living out the Truth is what gives the Gospel its greatest impact . . . showing people what real Life is all about. As a wiser man than I once said, "No one cares what you know until they know that you care." God knows this and thus wants us to live the Truth "exactly as commanded by the Father." That calls for diligence.

Far too many people live haphazardly from one day to the next. They do only what is needed to get by. Some put in just enough effort not to be fired, but nothing close to becoming "Employee of the Month." Far a vast majority of believers, they approach the faith in similar fashion – just enough to get to church (occasionally), but little or no further effort than that. Researchers have shared their insights into the faith-life of Christians in North America and it's abysmal! Fewer "believers" actually attend worship and fewer still participate in Bible study, discipleship training, fellowship, or service endeavors – the very marks of the early Church (cf. Acts 2:42ff). Many will try to place the onus on others: "Church is boring," and "I just don't get anything out of going to church." However, that thinking needs to be flipped: "You won't get anything out if you never put anything in: What are you investing in your church?"

Diligence. That seems to be the key that worked in Ephesus: "many members of your congregation are ***diligent*** in living out the Truth, exactly as commanded by the Father." Diligence is a constant and consistent effort, not an occasional fad. Daily Bible reading. Daily prayer time. Constant openness to living out the faith you claim to believe. Weekly worship with your believing brethren for mutual support and encouragement (which is called "edifying" or "edification"). Not just once-in-a-while; not just when it tickles your fancy. Daily. Purposefully. Diligently.

Prayer: Good and gracious God, every day You give us breath and bread; You are constant and steadfast in Your mercy and providence for us. You don't go on vacation and leave us to our own devices, but faithfully draw near to those who draw near to You. Give us a spirit of diligence. Moves us to engage daily in learning and living the Truth; through Jesus Christ, Your Son our Lord. Amen.

2 John 5, MSG

"But permit me a reminder, friends, and this is not a new commandment but simply a repetition of our original and basic charter: that we love each other. Love means following his commandments, and his unifying commandment is that you conduct your lives in love. This is the first thing you heard, and nothing has changed."

For John the Beloved – pastor, elder, apostle – at the end of the day everything about the Church focuses on and revolves around love. Love God. Love others. Love God by following His will. Love others as loved by God in Christ Jesus, which is His will for us. Agape-love. Selfless, sacrificial love. For John, the matter always seems to come back to this. It feels, to me, that the Upper Room experience of Maundy Thursday was engrained in John's psyche: the Master taking the role of lowly servant as He washes the disciple's grungy feet; Jesus' words explaining His example and commanding them to "love one another" in a manner that reflects to Christ's love for them: "this is not a new commandment but simply a repetition of our original and basic charter: that we love each other."

Imagine, though, what such love for others would look like in our churches. What if I set aside my personal preferences in order to help you in your journey rather than insist on "my way of the highway"? What would happen if the Body of Christ actually submitted itself to the Head of the Body rather than spend countless, wasted hours debating and arguing over color of carpet, whole wheat wafers, or two-ply toilet paper? Think of it: Selfless, sacrificial love that makes your needs more important than mine; everyone looking out for each other without worrying about themselves, knowing their brethren are covering their "six": I don't worry about me since that becomes your task; just as you no longer worry about you because I've taken on that job!

Love God by following His command out of thankful obedience; loving each other because that is His will for us in Christ. What a concept!

I have to let go of me to be able to help carry you. It's quite simple, really: "If it's all about Jesus (and it should be), it's not about me; if it's all about me, then it's not about Jesus!"

"Love means following his commandments and his unifying commandment is that you conduct your lives in love. This is the first thing you heard, and nothing has changed."

Prayer: Loved by Your deep, divine love in the Person and through the Work of Your only-begotten Son, move us to so love one another. Sometimes people can be so unlovable; but then, we, steeped in our sin and shame, were also – yet You loved us at the cross and love us today. Move us by Your love to love one another; through Jesus Christ our Lord. Amen.

2 John 7, MSG

"There are a lot of smooth-talking charlatans loose in the world who refuse to believe that Jesus Christ was truly human, a flesh-and-blood human being. Give them their true title: Deceiver! Antichrist!"

While theologians and commentaries have speculated over all the false narratives John was countering in his letters, the elder Apostle shares a specific, erroneous notion: those "who refuse to believe that Jesus Christ was truly human, a flesh-and-blood human being," Throughout the history of Christianity the "dual nature" of Jesus Christ (i.e., true God and true man) has probably been the most challenged and debated article of faith. Heretical propositions ranging from Jesus being "adopted" by God as a body for Him to use to Jesus only appearing to be a man have been put forward as answers to humankind's unwillingness to believe what God has to say about His only-begotten.

Addressing the matter of Christ's human nature, Scripture gives clear testimony. John speaks to the eternal presence of Jesus Christ when he writes in his Gospel account, "The Word became flesh and blood, and moved into the neighborhood. We saw the glory with our own eyes, the one-of-a-kind glory, like Father, like Son. Generous inside and out, true from start to finish."[73] Paul testifies that in Jesus "the whole fullness of deity dwells bodily."[74] and that "He appeared in a human body, was proved right by the invisible Spirit, was seen by the angels."[75] Paul gives us the reason for His human nature, telling the Galatians that "when the time that was set by God the Father, God sent his Son, born among us of a woman, born under the conditions of the law so that he might

[73] John 1:14, MSG.

[74] Colossians 2:9, ESV.

[75] 1 Timothy 3:16, MSG.

redeem those of us who have been kidnapped by the law."[76] We are told that "Since the children are made of flesh and blood, it's logical that the Savior took on flesh and blood in order to rescue them by his death."[77] It is the clear testimony of God's Word that His only-begotten Son, Jesus, took upon Himself our humanness in order to suffer and die for the salvation of humankind. Anyone proclaiming anything different? "Give them their true title: Deceiver! Antichrist!"

When we hear the word "antichrist," our imagination takes us to a devilish dictator dominating the world, wrestling humankind into an empire of great evil in opposition to the Church in the spirit of "The Omen" and other such horror movies. John doesn't picture such a character; elsewhere he speaks of "antichrists" roaming the world rather than a "boogey man." John portrays an "antichrist" as a "deceiver" – as someone who works to cast doubts and mislead people from the truth of God's Word. Anyone who maintains anything that goes against the clear Word of God – such as those who do not teach that Jesus Christ is true God and true man – such a person is an "antichrist" and is to be avoided.

Prayer: Lord, among us are charlatans, deceivers, and antichrists who seek to misinform and mislead the unsuspecting to doubt Your Word and to not believe what You say. Protect us from their influence; "Deliver us from evil." Direct our hearts and minds to the Scriptures lest their wicked speculations walk us straight into hell. Hear us for the sake of Your Son, our Lord – even Jesus Christ, true God and true man and Savior of the world. Amen.

---

[76] Galatians 4:4-5, MSG

[77] Hebrews 2:14, MSG.

2 John 8, MSG

"And be very careful around them so you don't lose out on what we've worked so diligently in together; I want you to get every reward you have coming to you."

"Just one more. You can do it. Suck it up. Good. Now let's do one more!"

Our strength and conditioning coach in High School was sometimes referred to as "Just One More Krejci," because no matter what you were doing in the weight room, he was always pushing. "Come on, now – you can do just one more!" That is the challenge in strength conditioning – that no matter how tired or how sore you may be, you keep trying to do that one more thing that will make you stronger and increase your endurance and stamina. Successful strength conditioning rests on pushing yourself to new limits so you can push yourself even farther. "Come on Mike, you can do just one more . . ." Coach's voice sometimes rings in my ears when contemplating throwing in the towel.

John is concerned about people hanging around the charlatans-deceivers-antichrist-types that began to infest the church. Anyone repeatedly listening to untruths will eventually begin to accept such notions as truth – or they will (at least) begin to doubt what they have believed. Continually battered by smooth talk and unreasonable dogmas made to sound reasonable, a person can become worn down. John says, "And be very careful around them so that you don't lose out…" Injury can take us out of the weight room or limit what we can do there; but therapy drives the recovering patient to exercise, strength conditioning, and endurance building. "Just one more. You can do it" becomes the mantra once again. John is challenging his readers not to give in, but to remain faithful to "what we've worked so diligently in together; I want you to get every reward you have coming to you."

Those charlatan-deceiver-antichrist-types are with us still today, opposing our long-held beliefs passed down from John and the rest of the holy evangelists for two millennia. The Scriptures speak God's Word in the face of their lies. But you have to keep going back to their witness like the athlete keeps going to the gym. It takes effort and discipline, but the payout comes through the Spirit's encouragement and blessing. "Come on. Just one more. You can do it!"

Prayer: "Almighty God, our heavenly Father, without Your help our labor is useless, and without Your light, our search is in vain. Invigorate our study of Your holy Word that, by due diligence and right discernment, we may establish ourselves and others in Your holy faith; through Jesus Christ our Lord. Amen."[78]

---

[78] *Lutheran Service Book,* Collect 203.

2 John 9, *MSG*

"Anyone who gets so progressive in his thinking that he walks out on the teaching of Christ, walks out on God. But whoever stays with the teaching, stays faithful to both the Father and the Son."

Increasingly, young Christian, Evangelical pastors are formally leaving Christianity to walk the paths of other religions, agnosticism, and humanism. For years they served as "professional Christians," as Bart Campolo (son of author and preacher Tony Campolo) puts it but nagging questions and their uncertainty regarding Biblical truth have led them to walk away from the Church. Marty Sampson, former worship leader for Hillsong United, issued a statement that reads (in part): "How can God be love yet send four billion people to a place, all 'coz they don't believe? No one talks about it. Christians can be the most judgmental people on the planet – they can also be some of the most beautiful and loving people. But it's not for me."

Other pastors – some deemed "successful pastors" by others – have simply called it "quits" after years of "running on empty," unable to manage the struggle to adapt to a "new normal" in culture and society. A young pastor recently quipped in passing, "There's nothing new for me to preach." To be certain, the world seems to have flipped on its head since 2020 pushed everyone and everything into panic mode and dismay; but worrying about preaching or teaching anything "new" or feeling like you're letting down people because you can't? That's placing a weight we were never designed or meant to carry. I don't convert or convince anyone; I share what I've been told, and the Spirit does the work – He does the heavy lifting. So, as my father would say, "Sometimes it's best to stick with what 'brung' ya' this far."

"Anyone who gets so progressive in his thinking that he walks out on the teaching of Christ, walks out on God." The Good News of Jesus Christ may very well be "old news," but it's good "old news." Just because I've averaged 60-plus sermons a year for almost forty years doesn't mean I've shared everything there is to share. Every time I go to the Scriptures, the Spirit leads me into deeper truths; and maybe I am led to share a "new" thought, but most often I am led to share the Gospel in a little different way than I have before. My job is to dig; God delivers up the gold when it comes to the Bible. I could preach the Gospel every day and still find people who haven't heard it the first time. God's faithfulness, our sin, mercy, repentance, grace, faith, salvation, restoration, new life – all the elements of the Gospel speak tons to sinful children of men who forget, deny, rebel, suffer, sorrow, repent, seek God's forgiveness, hear absolution, and repeat. To walk away from the Gospel of Jesus Christ is to walk away from God Himself – and there's definitely nothing new about that! "But whoever stays with the teaching, stays faithful to both the Father and the Son."

The wisdom writer once said, "There is nothing new under the sun."[79] The constant of the Bible is the steadfast love and faithfulness of God in His promise of Messiah, the coming of Messiah, and the salvation wrought by Messiah-Jesus on the cross. The teaching is timeless and transcends the thoughts and fancies of men – what could ever "progress" beyond the grace of God?

Prayer: Sometimes, Lord, we look at life as a tired, old joke with a repetitive punchline that garners no laughs and feels out-of-date. But what sweeter sound or heart-warming words are there than the Gospel? Keep us as faithful to the Good News as You are toward us in Your love and righteousness; through Jesus Christ our Savior. Amen.

---

[79] Ecclesiastes 1:9, MSG.

2 John 10-11, *MSG*

"If anyone shows up who doesn't hold to this teaching, don't invite him in and give him the run of the place. That would just give him a platform to perpetuate his evil ways, making you his partner."

An older pastor once told me, "You may want to check out a guest speaker *before* you let him step up to your pulpit." Like many of us, this pastor had agreed to let a guest evangelist speak to his people one Sunday, and within the opening minutes of the sermon regretted his decision. "It took me weeks to calm my people down and to apologize for some of the things he said!" I've likewise allowed the occasional guest preacher to speak, grimacing at things they said and regretting my decision.

John addresses the allowance of a false teacher to peddle his false narrative in a congregation. Christians tend to be gracious people, even when they shouldn't be. While we strive to be courteous and nonabrasive in our demeanor, there are times and circumstances when we cannot be open to certain people and what they're peddling. I've been asked to speak kindly toward groups or allow a presentation to be shared about an "opportunity" that wanted to "help" my people, but in a questionable manner. I've politely (and, sometimes, not-so-politely) said, "No." It's hard to close the door once it's been opened wide. "If anyone shows up who doesn't hold to this teaching, don't invite him in and give him the run of the place."

My Lutheran tribe is a confessional church-body. Along with the historic creeds – Apostles', Nicene, Athanasian – our Reformation-fathers clearly stated what we "believe, teach, and confess" from the Scriptures in a series of confessions. The Bible is God's Word – period. The confessions are clear expositions of what the Scriptures teach and how we live out our faith in a

God-pleasing way. My tribe lives in agreement with the Scriptures and the Lutheran Confessions as a way to measure our words and teachings as well as to think through and respond to the teachings of others. Probably not as loving as we should be at times, we staunchly maintain our mutually agreed-upon faith and practice of the "teaching of Jesus Christ." To do differently "would just give him a platform to perpetuate his evil ways, making [us] his partner."

Prayer: While we want to embrace all believers as brethren in Jesus Christ, O Lord, we ask You to give us the discernment to listen carefully and measure peoples' words according to Your Word. Give us Your Spirit to gently speak to those willing to hear and the courage to oppose false teaching in our midst. Keep us faithful unto all eternity; through Jesus Christ our Lord. Amen.

2 John 12-13, MSG

"I have a lot more things to tell you, but I'd rather not use paper and ink. I hope to be there soon in person and have a heart-to-heart talk. That will be far more satisfying to both you and me. Everyone here in your sister congregation sends greetings."

Our children and grandchildren are scattered across the country – literally coast-to-coast. We don't get the opportunity to personally visit them very often. We have to settle for phone calls and the occasional "Facetime" video-chat. These newer forms of communication obviously surpass the days of pen-and-paper letters that could take weeks to receive via "snail-mail." But there's nothing that compares to "being there" when it comes to family and friends!

John is hoping for an end to his forced absence from the congregation he loves. From the correspondence he was receiving it seems he was desperately needed back in Ephesus: "I have a lot more things to tell you, but I'd rather not use paper and ink." Being the elder Apostle and good pastor that he was, John was truly concerned for his people. Deceivers and antichrists with their peculiar notions and false narratives were obviously continuing to question and challenge "the teaching of Christ." Perhaps they were swaying more believers to doubt or even abandon the faith. Letters weren't hacking it. "I hope to be there soon in person and have a heart-to-heart talk. That will be far more satisfying to both you and me." Letters, emails, texts – even chatrooms and remote meetings – cannot replace the power and the effect of in-person gatherings of God's people. "I hope to be there soon," he pines. "We need to talk."

Talking as brothers and sisters to brothers and sisters does not happen as much as it should. Churches have replaced earnest conversations with meetings, programs, and organized fellowship events that may fill our schedules, but leave empty the hole in our hearts that yearn for more. "Church" for too many has become an event rather than an experience shared by brethren coming together at the gracious invitation of God. We come. We sit. We're often more entertained than convicted. We go home. We've read the text, replied with an emoji, and then deleted the thread. Sometimes we may chat for a few moments but soon scamper off to our waiting chariots to go to the next event on our weekend itineraries. John's yearning to be with his fellow believers can be lost to us: "I hope to be there soon . . . That will be far more satisfying to both you and me."

Take the time and the advantage of the opportunities available to gather for worship; but extend the experience to be with your fellow believers, sharing in the mutual consolation of the saints. Talk to one another. Embrace what you share with each other – Christ. Grace. Faith. Hope. Love. "Everyone here in your sister congregation sends greetings."

Prayer: We feel alone – detached from and disconnected as a people, O God. Sometimes we may feel disenfranchised or distant even from You! We fail to talk. We don't share what we have or who we are – with You or anyone else. Gather us under Your wings, O Lord, and bring us together at the invitation of Your grace. Encourage us to receive and share Your love with one another that together we may be no longer lonely or lost, but one in You and with You; through Jesus Christ, Your Son, and our Savior. Amen.

3 John 1-4, MSG

"The Pastor, to my good friend Gaius: How truly I love you! We're the best of friends, and I pray good fortune in everything you do, and for your good health - that your everyday affairs prosper, as well as your soul! I was most happy when some friends arrived and brought the news that you persist in following the way of Truth. Nothing could make me happier than getting reports that my children continue diligently in the way of Truth!"

Having four children, we had a brood who had a broad spectrum of interests and activities and who went off in all directions in their individual lives. They chose different directions to go and different things to do. Each of them is unique and it has been interesting, watching them become who they are today. Beyond what they've done and are doing is how they live out their values. Some of the values as hoped we had modeled for them have become evident in the lives and decisions. For the most point they've become people God is, can, and will use for the sake of His kingdom.

Gaius was considered a "good friend" among those John called his "children." He was evidently successful and used his blessings from God well. John prays for continued personal and spiritual success. But what was it that made the apostle "happy"? "I was most happy when some friends arrived and brought the news that you persist in following the way of Truth. Nothing could make me happier than getting reports that my children continue diligently in the way of Truth." Just as parents beam with a sense of pride over the children's accomplishments, the elder Apostle gushes over the diligence of his "children" in their faith-walk with Jesus Christ.

Setting the good example and modeling the values you want to impart to your children should be uppermost on the heart and mind of a parent. John had worked diligently to teach his people about Jesus and the "way of Truth," and Gaius served to illustrate that his efforts had a modicum of success. Children tend to follow their parents' lead – both good and bad. Parents set the example for their children to emulate. The values of the original household often become the values (or, at least part of the values) of succeeding households. If the "way of Truth" is taught from parents to children, they can also be taught from children to grandchildren; but if not, the "way of Truth" meets a "dead end," and it is the succeeding generations who suffer.

For the sake of our children and grandchildren we all should seek to walk in the "way of Truth" and model the faith for both this generation and the generation to come!

Prayer: "Almighty God, heavenly Father, You have blessed us with the joy and care of children. Give us calm strength and patient wisdom that, as they grow in years, we may teach them to love whatever is just and true, following the good example of our Savior, Jesus Christ, our Lord. Amen." [LSB, Collect 246]

3 John 5, MSG

"Dear friend, when you extend hospitality to Christian brothers and sisters, even when they are strangers, you make the faith visible."

Have you ever visited a different church while on a trip or during vacation? Over the years we have, and the experiences have varied greatly. I've noticed, for instance, when I visited in some sort of "official" capacity I was received more respectfully than when I attended less conspicuously. At one of those "official" visits, I entered the building with my clerical collar on, trying to carry my notes and vestments bag. Ushers immediately sprang to my assistance and "oozed" greetings of welcome all over me. Meanwhile, my wife, who was a few steps behind me (we often walk in separately to see how each of us will be received), entered and not a single person acknowledged her presence! While on vacation – especially when our four children were young – we would arrive and, more-times-than-not, be greeted with glares and contempt. ("Oh, great, more squiggly, noisy kids!") We'd sit down and even had people get up and move a couple of pews away from us. But – and I want to say this clearly – we were also greeted at times with the warmest of receptions, even when no one knew that I was a pastor. I will have to say that the way we were greeted (or, not) made a tremendous difference for our worship experience!

While people aren't supposed to go to a church looking for a warm greeting and loving welcome (after all, we go to worship God, not to be worshiped), hospitality is something everyone should receive. In the Old Testament, God's people are repeatedly directed to welcome the stranger and the sojourner since they, too, had once been travelers. If we are as loving as we are called to be by God ("love one another even as I have loved you" – Jesus), then showing hospitality and welcome to people shouldn't be much of a challenge. If someone "new" or even "strange" enters the building, God probably had something to do with getting them there; it's up to you to welcome them and make them feel at home. Scripture puts it this way: "Let brotherly love continue. Do not neglect show hospitality to strangers, for thereby some have entertained angels unawares."[80]

To be sure, COVID-19 has tempered the warmth of extending greetings: "fist bumps" have replaced warm handshakes and hugs. But hospitality can (and should) still be shown, even at a "social distance." Where there's a will, there's a way, right? Even if you cannot "Greet one another with a holy kiss."[81], that is no excuse for not being hospitable and welcoming in the Lord.

Prayer: I saw them enter, Lord, but I didn't want to extend a greeting; I just wanted to find my pew and sit down. Perhaps someone else greeted them, but maybe not. Anyway, I failed You when I failed to greet them as guests in my Father's house. Forgive me for my callousness and encourage my sense of hospitality, taking the time and making the effort to "extend hospitality to Christian brothers and sisters, even when they are strangers," that I can "make the faith visible" as a loving and faithful disciple; through Jesus Christ my Lord. Amen.

---

[80] Hebrews 13:1-2, ESV.

[81] 1 Corinthians 16:20, ESV.

3 John 6-9, MSG

"They've made a full report back to the church here, a message about your love. It's good work you're doing, helping these travelers on their way, hospitality worthy of God himself! They set out under the banner of the Name, and get no help from unbelievers. So they deserve any support we can give them. In providing meals and a bed, we become their companions in spreading the Truth."

I can remember as a teenager when a missionary family came to my home church. They had spent their third, three-year assignment in Africa and were home on furlough. While they were taking a "rest" from their mission work, they were also traveling to churches and circuit areas of our Lutheran tribe, securing commitments for their return to the mission field. They set up their displays with tribal trinkets and clothes, books filled with pictures – even a slide carousel projector for pictures on a screen during Bible class. The mission pastor preached, a special collection was taken up and a three-year commitment to support them was secured. My home church, regardless of their shortcomings, was supportive of world missions and missionaries.

Earlier we heard John warn the church not to let just anyone in (2 John 10ff) since false teachers were also traveling about. The criteria specified then is reiterated here: the litmus test of "the teaching of Christ" and "the Church" is referred to as these true evangelists traveling "under the banner of the Name" – Jesus Christ. Just as believers weren't to open their doors to the false teachers who traveled about, they were to receive, welcome, and support the evangelist-missionaries who came through: "So they deserve any support we can give them. In providing meals and a bed, we become their companions in spreading the Truth."

While most missionaries use the internet and well-produced newsletters to garner support and appraise their constituents regarding their work and what God is up to in other parts of the world, they need the support of their family of faith. I take my hat off to foreign missionaries. They willingly give up the comforts of living in America to go to remote regions, face difficult physical and medical conditions, and even expose themselves to violence and terrorism from those opposed to the Gospel. They do it all for the sake of people who, otherwise, might never hear the Good News of Jesus Christ, the Lord and Savior of us all. "It's good work you're doing, helping these travelers on their way, hospitality worthy of God himself!"

Prayer: Holy God and heavenly Father, we lift up our thanks and praise that You have equipped, empowered, and enable men and women to serve in foreign mission fields. Move us to support such work with our prayers and gifts that they may suffer no want or need unmet even as they serve You in their missionary work. Hear us as we pray in the name of our Savior, Jesus Christ, our Lord. Amen.

3 John 9-10, MSG

"Earlier I wrote something along this line to the church, but Diotrephes, who loves being in charge, denigrates my counsel. If I come, you can be sure that I'll hold him to account for spreading vicious rumors about us. As if that weren't bad enough, he not only refuses hospitality to traveling Christians but tries to stop others from welcoming them. Worse yet, instead of inviting them in he throws them out."

Sir John Dalberg-Action is credited as the one who wrote, "Power tends to corrupt, and absolute power corrupts absolutely." Too often men, when placed in charge, allow their promotions to go to their heads; what's worse is when they *think* they're in charge and begin to assert their unfounded authority! So full of themselves, such tyrants try to rule with an iron fist and impose their will upon their charges. Like under such self-appointed dictators is most difficult, to be sure.

Without anything more than the context of these two verses we can suppose that Diotrephes was such a person. Whether he was actually "in charge" or not, the elder Apostle posits that he "loves being in charge," but that he is not modeling the type of servant-leadership John had learned from Jesus. The Lord set the example by washing His disciples' gross, grimy, grubby feet. "Do you understand what I have done to you? You address me as 'Teacher' and 'Master,' and rightly so. This is what I am. So if I, the Master and Teacher, washed your feet, you must now wash each other's feet. I've laid down a pattern for you. What I've done, you do. I'm only pointing out the obvious. A servant is not ranked above his master; an employee doesn't give orders to the employer. If you understand what I'm telling you, act like it – live a blessed life."[82] Diotrephes was not modeling the kind of leadership that should have been on display; John would be addressing this with him at some point.

[82] John 13:12-17, MSG.

It takes courage to lead like Jesus. His example is one of service and sacrifice rather than that of authority and compulsion. Thankfully, most who serve "in the name and by the command of Christ" do follow His pattern, but occasionally, we find those like Diotrephes – loving that they're "in charge," but ruling rather than serving as they should. Don't follow Diotrephes' example as you serve the Lord and His people!

Prayer: Lord, if You have placed me in charge, please fill me with Your Spirit that I see the opportunity as one of service and not as ruling over others. You set the example in the Upper Room and upon the Cross: Let me walk in Your footsteps with my words and by my deeds; to the glory and praise of Your name. Amen.

3 John 11, MSG

"Friend, don't go along with evil. Model the good. The person who does good does God's work. The person who does evil falsifies God, doesn't know the first thing about God.

Did you ever get into trouble because one of your "supposed" friends talked you into doing something that you knew better than to do? Haven't we all? Maybe it was a prank that backfired or went horribly wrong. Perhaps you were talked into holding a bottle rocket while someone else lit it; or you stuck your tongue to a metal pole on an exceptionally cold winter's day because you were "double-dog-dared" to. Whenever I did something that someone else talked me into I can still hear my mother (with hands on her hips and her head cocked to one side) ask, "And if they'd told you to jump off a cliff, you would have – right?"

What usually resulted from going along with stupidity (embarrassment, injury, ridicule) is worse when you go along with evil. History is replete with stories of leaders and nations negotiating with evil regimes only to find themselves at war anyway (e.g., Neville Chamberlain's doctrine of "appeasement" toward Nazi Germany didn't stop World War II). Evil is not satiated with compromise; it doesn't stop until it gets what it wants. Going along with evil, though you hope to lessen the impact, only serves to worsen you; all you accomplish is becoming evil's partner.

"Friend, don't go long with evil. Model the good." Having addressed and commended his readers regarding "the Truth" and their hospitality to other believers, John has a simple plan for dealing with evil. It consisted of one, simple step: Don't! "The person who does evil falsifies God, doesn't know the first thing about God." There are no "white lies" or "innocent half-truths" out there; no shades of morality that appear to be helpful or expedient. "The person who does good does God's work." Yes . . . life can be (and often is) just that simple. Trying to work with people who have evil intent only serves to allow them to creep ever closer to their endgame. Leonardo da Vinci is quoted as saying, "He who does not oppose evil . . . commands it to be done."

Prayer: "Almighty and everlasting God, through Your Son You have promised us forgiveness of sins and everlasting life. Govern our hearts by Your Holy Spirit that in our daily need, and especially in time of temptation, we may seek Your help and, by a true and lively faith in Your Word, obtain all that You have promised; through the same Jesus Christ our Lord. Amen."[83]

[83] *Lutheran Service Book*, Collect 209.

3 John 12, MSG

"Everyone has a good word for Demetrius - the Truth itself stands up for Demetrius! We concur, and you know we don't hand out endorsements lightly."

Have you ever considered what people will have to say about you when you die? What will be the legacy you leave; for what might you be remembered? As we get older, the thought crosses one's mind.

The story is told about Sir Alfred Nobel, a chemist who, among other things, invented dynamite and converted Bofors into a major arnaments producer. The story goes that one morning, as he read his morning paper, he happened upon his obituary which had erroneously reported his death. As he read the obituary, he came to realize that his legacy would be one only of death and destruction. It had dubbed him "the angel of death." His other discoveries were over-shadowed and forgotten. He immediately set about to change the end of his story, creating a foundation, and funding it to recognize achievements in a variety of fields – most notably, the Nobel Peace Prize. He wanted people not to think of him as "the angel of death," but as a humanitarian and benefactor to the arts and sciences.

Of the hundreds and thousands of believers at the end of the First Century AD and the Apostolic Era (which would end with John's death), precious few are mentioned by name. Demetrius is honored to be named in the Bible. It seems that his life was a "stand-out" testimony to his faith: "Everyone has a good word for Demetrius – the Truth itself stands up for Demetrius! We concur, and you know we don't hand out endorsements lightly."

Approaching one's inevitable end at funeral and graveside, it is a worthy endeavor to consider your legacy as a testimony to the

Lord Jesus Christ. After all, as Paul speaks of his life under the cross, he submits, "Indeed, I have been crucified with Christ. My ego is no longer central. It is no longer important that I appear righteous before you or have your good opinion, and I am no longer driven to impress God. Christ lives in me. The life you see me living is not 'mine,' but it is lived by faith in the Son of God, who loved me and gave himself for me. I am not going to go back on that."[84]

At the end of the journey, what really matters is what God has to say: "Good servant! Great work!."[85]

Prayer: It will all come to an end someday, Lord, when my journey ends, my heart ceases to beat, and I draw my last breath. My tombstone will have the date of my birth and the date of my death, separated by a "dash." May all that happens in that "dash" honor you among those who have known me; through Jesus Christ, my Lord and my Savior. Amen.

---

[84] Galatians 2:19-20, MSG.

[85] Luke 19:17, MSG.

3 John 13-15, MSG

"I have a lot more things to tell you, but I'd rather not use pen and ink, I hope to be there soon in person and have a heart-to-heart talk. Peace to you. The friends here say hello. Greet our friends there by name."

St. John the Beloved, the last remaining evangelist and apostle of Jesus Christ closes his correspondence with two wishes: that he would return to Ephesus and to his friends in person, and that his congregation would have "peace." There seems to be some patristic evidence that he was allowed to return from Patmos, but some doubts prevail as to that notion. What we do know is that John had an abiding concern for those to whom he wrote. He longed to return to them; he had things he wanted to say to them in person rather than writing them down. And he wanted them to have peace – "Peace to you" he writes.

PEACE. In days of stress and anxiety, wouldn't a little "peace" be nice? As we think of it in terms of the word's common usage, we'd all like a little "peace and quiet" and yearn for "peace like a river." Biblical "peace" is much more.

The concept of Biblical "peace" comes from the Hebrew "shalom" in the Old Testament and "eirene" from the Greek language of the New Testament. Biblical "peace" is more than just the cessation of hostilities; it is more focused on taking action to restore brokenness among humankind. The goal is not a sense of inner tranquility but a state of wholeness and completion. It's not something we create but is a gift of the Holy Spirit. Ultimately, "peace" is all about relationships – whether between God and humanity or man-to-man. It may require repentance, reconciliation, and restoration through forgiveness, and a desire to set right any wrong committed. In its simplest terms, Biblical "peace" takes what is broken and puts it back together.

"Peace to you," the elder apostles writes, "The friends here say hello. Greet our friends there by name." John looks forward to being back with those he'd been separated from. What had been broken by forced separation was to be restored – that's his fervent hope and desire. "Peace to you."

Prayer: "O God, from whom came all holy desires, all good counsels, and all just works, give to us, Your servants, that peace which the world cannot give, that our hearts may be set to obey Your commandments and also that we, being defended from the fear of our enemies, may live in peace and quietness; through Jesus Christ, Your Son, our Lord, who lives and reigns with You and the Holy Spirit, one God, now and forever. Amen."[86]

---

[86] *Lutheran Service Book,* Collect 410.